Narcissism

Escape From a Codependent Relationship and Deal With a Narcissistic With Confidence

(Learning to Find Peace After a Toxic Relationship With Antisocial and Psychopaths)

Ellen Aniston

Published By **Jordan Levy**

Ellen Aniston

All Rights Reserved

Narcissism: Escape From a Codependent Relationship and Deal With a Narcissistic With Confidence (Learning to Find Peace After a Toxic Relationship With Antisocial and Psychopaths)

ISBN 978-1-998769-03-2

No part of this guidebook shall be reproduced in any form without permission in writing from the publisher except in the case of brief quotations embodied in critical articles or reviews.

Legal & Disclaimer

The information contained in this ebook is not designed to replace or take the place of any form of medicine or professional medical advice. The information in this ebook has been provided for educational & entertainment purposes only.

The information contained in this book has been compiled from sources deemed reliable, and it is accurate to the best of the Author's knowledge; however, the Author cannot guarantee its accuracy and validity and cannot be held liable for any errors or omissions. Changes are periodically made to this book. You must consult your doctor or get professional medical advice before using

Table Of Contents

Chapter 1: What You Need To Know About Narcissism and Gaslighting?

Gaslighting is an expression of manic behavior that has its roots in the 1944 film Gaslight. This movie tells of a man who manipulates and abuses his wife to drive her insane.

Perverse narcissists or psychopaths, by gaslighting, will deny or affirm that events have occurred. They will then claim they have said sentences that were never spoken or claimed that they have never told speeches. The victim could be at grave risk of their mental health being compromised.

Phase one - the victim has enough faith in his memory and perception to continue the process. The victim attempts to make the perverted, deranged narcissist think, but he is confused, incredulous, shocked, and perplexed. Also, the distorted speeches start with "the speech must have been distorted so that victims do not understand the destructive process and why it is becoming increasingly confused." The victim will be less likely to become impotent if they are deprived of the truth. (Hirigoyen 2000).

Second phase: The defense of the victim starts even if unconscious. The victim argues animatedly and fights with the malignant neurotic narcissist. He then tries desperately to persuade the psychopath to invest every psychic or emotional resource to improve the relationship. But at this point, he will silence, verbal violence and disappearances and the victim will fear abandonment.

Third stage – The victim may experience depression, mental or physical health problems. When she begins to see that all attempts are futile and history is not a success, she loses confidence in herself. She will eventually believe that the executioner served her was righteous, authentic, just, and deserved. At this point, it is very easy to descend into hell.

This powerful and dangerous technique can be used in a fixed pattern. It is also used with the triangulation. Gaslighting occurs slowly and almost unnoticeably. Most victims of gaslighting will be able, once they are educated about the malignant psychopath and narcissist, to understand the process. However, they won't be able, or even remember, when the abuse began.

The gaslighter will resort to this system even in small, insignificant, and apparently insignificant things. I have never revealed to you that my mom likes pastries. Are you kidding? It is true that he has diabetes. Perhaps your ex's mom or lover loves pastries! Evidently, the pathologically obsessed narcissist had actually told the victim her mother loved sweets. He never even mentioned diabetes to her. Conversations like this, which are repeated at fixed times on different topics, create in the victim a confusional condition, a distrust and a lack of confidence in his abilities of perception, memory, and observation.

You can fall for this type of behavior. It is very common among dictators and cult leader, as well as abusers.

This kind of abuse is slow-doped so the victim is unaware of the brainwashing that he is going through.

Gaslighting can also be used to tell lies but they are adept at hiding them. The manipulator will "overturn the deck" so it is easy to believe that the truth is being reported.

The manipulators may then try to discredit what was said. The victim starts to doubt himself as he accepts the reality of the other, and this cycle will continue for many more years.

Abusers also know how to strike, and they can attack anything that is precious.

When children are present, they accuse each other as being incapable and deserving.

They established a type of "psychological terrorist" to take down basic securities. The intent was to make each other vulnerable.

How can the prey fail to see what is happening? How can he possibly not be aware gaslighting, triangulation and violence? I need help understanding it so I ask for help from an analogy: the story of a boiled frog.

John Hopkins University, 1882, conducted research that led to the discovery and phenomenon of the boiled Frog. One experiment revealed that when Americans threw a frog into boiling water, the frog jumped to safety. In contrast, placing the frog into a pot of cold and slowly heating it, made the frog boil. This experiment shows how our nervous system works.

Every time we make a major change in our lives, the brain, just like the frog that boils in boiling water, tries to go back to its old ways, cancelling any attempts at change. If violence, betrayal or lies, gaslighting, or other extreme acts were to become immediately obvious, then victims would flee. In order to achieve lasting change, and to undermine healthy escape reactions, the malignant psychopath and narcissist use the only truly effective technique. It involves introducing small changes, micro traumas, but it is not permanent. .

These tiny changes may be invisible to our nervous system for the short term but will result in paralysis long term. When the victim realizes what he is going through, he will be so weak, damaged, or prostrate that it will be impossible for him to jump from the boiling water. It is important to recall that manipulators alternate violent with gratifying praises, adding an extra level of confusion to prey's perceptions of what they perceive and how they remember it.

To make it easier for others to withdraw, the perverse narcissist/psychopath will also tell others that you are insane. You will be told by the psychopath that everyone around you, including your relatives and friends, is lying. This will again lead to questions about your reality.

How do you defend yourself? Through information. It is important to note down all conversations and statements at the beginning. The pervert wants you only to turn to him.

They are intended to make it difficult for you to believe in yourself. Your executioner is using cruel manipulative techniques called gaslighting against your.

It is the most popular invisible weapon of manipulators, psychological violators. It is the subtlest form of psychological violence. Although it does not leave any wounds on the body, it leaves bruises on your soul. Gaslighters may be family members, friends, coworkers, bosses, and partners.

The gaslighter alters your perception of reality. They will lead you to believe that a lie can be the truth. You may believe that you are crazy. All with the sole purpose of destroying your judgement capacity, creating an underlying insecurity, and making you dependent on him. This manipulative strategy can even cause serious psychological consequences to the victim.

Here are the differences between gaslighting methods:

Denial is when the malignant narcissist/psychopathic gaslighter refuses listening or pretends not understanding what you have to say.

These dysfunctional dynamics can lead to a spiral of mental and emotional confusion that will ultimately lead to depression.

The game is over. After the love bombing phase, the psychopaths and the perverse neurotic will use sarcasms and criticism only occasionally. However, over time, the criticisms will become more vicious and insistent. The victim, however, will become more dependent on the partner, as a result of gaslighting and fear of the treatment of silence.

It is essential to understand that violence is happening to you. Pay attention to the alarms and write down the phrases. If they keep coming up, consider ending the relationship.

You will also need to rebuild your self-confidence regardless of the extent of damage. Once you realize that this is manipulation and that the problem is not in you, but in your emotions and memory, you can remember that gaslighter attacks are a psychological abuse tactic.

Remember that your emotions, your feelings, are valid and true. That certain expressions are used only by the gaslighter to harm you. Trust your memory.

Gaslighting victims experience the following symptoms:

Ask yourself constant questions

Trust your instincts. Trust your memory. Trust your intuitions. Trust your intuitions. Trust your feelings of pain. Trust your pain: If you are suffering from them, it's likely that someone is hurting. Trust your anger. Trust your confusion. Someone is trying to confuse or confuse you.

Never lose sight of your values.

Trusting yourself is more important than trusting someone else.

Chapter 2: Narcissistic Abuse

Abuse comes in many forms. Most of them leave no mark on the victim's body. All types of abuse can still leave the victim in pain at the hands of their abuser. No matter the form of abuse, this kind of treatment is unacceptable and should not be allowed.

There is a cyclical element to all types of abuse. This means that there are four distinct stages which will continue to occur until something changes. Tensions build in the first step. This stage can lead to communication difficulties, fear and a feeling of being victimized. The incident is the second stage. The incident would take place regardless of the abuse in the relationship. This stage is often dominated by the abuser, who will be angry at the victim and threaten to continue abuse if they don't get their way. Step three is reconciliation. In this stage, the abuser apologizes for his actions and promises not to repeat them. The abuser often promises to be safer while subtly blaming their victim. Once the victim has given up, they will move on to step 4. Step four refers to the period of calmness following the incident, where there is no abuse. This is also known as the honeymoon period, where everything is happy. This is the time the victim lives for. The victim forgives the abuser to return to this stage of life and continue the cycle.

Types of Narcissistic Abusement

To get victims to follow his lead, the narcissist might use several types of abuse. These abuses shouldn't be ignored or downplayed because they aren't obvious. A red flag that indicates you may be being abused should also be raised immediately. If abuse is suspected, it's important that you contact local domestic violence agencies, particularly if you are unable to stop the abuse yourself.

Abuse of the physical

This is the most common definition of abuse. The punishments for physical abuse are those that involve the use of physical force. Anything that causes you to feel pain or discomfort, no matter how small, is considered physical abuse. Any time that another party has touched your skin in any way, whether it was by touching you directly or placing a hand on you, it should be reported as physical abuse. Your body is yours alone to govern. You can choose not to be touched.

One lesser-known aspect to physical abuse is that it can keep you physically bound. Physical abuse can also be committed if the abuser prevents you from leaving an area. You may be subject to abuse if another person takes your phone away from you in order to stop your ability call for help. Abuse that has become physical should be stopped as soon as it can be.

Verbal Abuse

Verbally abusing someone verbally is when their voice is in any way meant to hurt you or degrade your character. Belittling, disparaging comments or yelling at someone are examples of verbally abusive remarks. While others may criticize you, but they legitimately use them to benefit you, the narcissist uses her voice to keep you down.

Oft, verbal abuse is ignored since it does not leave a permanent mark. However, constant insulting and name calling can wear down your mental well-being and cause long-term damage.

Verbal abuse refers to any kind of verbal harm including threats, demands or guilt trips, sarcasm and yelling.

Sexual Abuse

One of the most harmful and dangerous forms of abuse is sexual abuse. Sexual abuse can be defined as forced sexual acts or inappropriate sexual touch without consent.

You don't have to have full intercourse. Just touching your skin in an unwelcome way or tapping your genitals without your consent is considered sexual abuse.

You should remember that even though you might be in a romantic relationship or are married to the other person, this does not mean you have permission to use parts of your body in ways you do not agree with.

If sexual contact is not consented to, one spouse can abuse the other. Anyone under the influence drugs or alcohol can not consent to sexual contact or sleeping. This is also known as sexual abuse.

Financial Abuse

You are often denied money if you are the victim of financial abuse. This is most common in abusive relationships. One person usually stays at home and the other earns all of capital. But this is not always true. The money is controlled by one person and the access to it is restricted, regardless of who makes it. The whole point of this is to keep the dependent reliant on the abuser to meet all their needs.

This often involves multiple bank accounts being used to restrict access. The victim receives either nothing or very small amounts of money at one time to cover basic necessities and withhold the rest. You may have been robbed of your money or the abuser might have moved all your funds into an account they don't have. It is possible to be a victim of financial abuse by getting credit cards in your name. This will allow you to incur debt and keep trapped. You could be a victim financial abuse if your spouse does not allow you equal access to the money and you refuse to agree to such an arrangement. While some couples do decide to separate their finances, this must be mutually decided.

Emotional Abuse

Emotional abuse aims to hurt you emotionally. This can include threats to keep you on your toes, the silent treatment to make you feel hurt, and belittling you. These manipulation attempts are designed to play with your emotions in order to entertain the narcissist. As manipulation attempts try to sway you through appealing to emotions, most fall under this category.

Neglect

Neglect isn't just limited to parent-child dynamics. However, it can also occur in other situations where the victim is being taken care of by the narcissist. Neglect occurs when the person in control does not provide what the dependent needs to live and thrive. This could mean that the person in power does not provide what the dependent needs to live and thrive. If the narcissist holds all the money in a relationship, financial abuse could occur. This could occur if the other person is not provided with what they require or has the means to pay for it.

Isolation

As a form of emotional abuse, isolation can also be used to prevent victim from being able to reach out to others who could support him. This may include making it difficult for others to approach the victim, making it uncomfortable for family members and friends to visit, and restricting contact via social media.

If the narcissist insists you stop talking to certain people if your relationship is going on, you are likely being manipulated.

There are many types if Narcissists

While they may share many characteristics with each other, Narcissists typically fall within one of three categories. They can be overtly, covertly, or toxic. These narcissists still fall within the criteria of a narcissist. However, they exhibit different behaviors.

The obvious are often quite talented, but the hidden ones tend to be more secretive and narcissistic. Toxic Narcissists tend to be the most extreme outliers. They want to inflict pain and suffering on as many people as possible just to make them feel bad. Understanding the behavior patterns of narcissists is key to recognizing when they are not. You will be able to understand more about narcissists so that you can better deal with them.

The Covert Narcissist

Covert, also known by vulnerable narcissists (or simply covert), are very discreet about their manipulation techniques. Because they feel abandoned or rejected, they hide behind the victim mask. They try to use fear of rejection as a motivator to get others to support them. To make it easier to maintain their circle, the best way is to pretend they are receiving more help. People are more inclined than others to help people who have suffered trauma or are suffering from emotional distress. This is the reason for the covert narcissist's tendency to victimhood.

The covert, narcissist can feel inferiority or superiority depending upon what happened in the past. In order to feel superior, they turn to narcissistic support, making themselves the victim of their circumstances in order get what they desire. After they have taken advantage of someone else's attention, it is possible to feel superior again.

Covert Narcissists can be quite reactive. They can't cope with the unexpected. If they aren't given what they desire, they will explode. It is clear that the covert, or narcissist, can be very violent and aggressive if provoked. They may prefer to pretend to be victims in all situations but when they start to feel overwhelmed they have to take off the mask, which exposes their real vulnerability and allows them to show their authentic self.

When challenged, the covert-narcissist begins to exhibit passive aggression to try and remain the victim. If possible, the covert Narcissist will continue to maintain this persona. Consider this: Your spouse may be a covertly narcissist who arrives home from work late and leaves you scrambling to get there on time. In such a case, you might tell her to call you if it is likely that she will be late. Then you can plan accordingly and schedule alternative care. Your narcissistic spouse will likely start to cry about how much you do not trust her, and how hard she tries to care for the family. She's so busy working and trying to make more money, she forgets she can be a reliable partner.

Now, you have to take on the responsibility. You have two options. Either tell her she isn't stupid, giving validation to her victim mentality, OR you refuse and risk setting her off on a narcissistic rampage. Both of these options are not ideal, which is the general theme with the narcissist. The best strategy is to not play.

The covert narcissist, in the end is quite fragile. She is so concerned about her self consciousness that she pretends to not be. This is the self she creates. She is, in essence overcompensating and creating false self to make her appear more confident than herself.

She is driven to build relationships with people, but her inability and unwillingness to empathize effectively means she has trouble making any meaningful connections. This makes her self-worth dependent on other people validating her. To increase her self-esteem she needs to feel supported and loved by others. She attempts to build a relationship with others.

Typically, the covert personality is the result from childhood trauma. She may feel abandoned or neglected and creates a persona of perfection to hide the fact that she didn't cause the abuse, neglect, abandonment or other traumas.

The vulnerable narcissist's goal is far more realistic than the grandiose narcissist, who seeks to be the center attention and be considered superior to all.

She wants to be the best at whatever role she's in and someone that is respected by everyone. She doesn't need to hold the ultimate power to be recognized and appreciated for the effort she puts into her work. She is more interested in being seen as a great mom, wife, friend, or community member than being in a leadership role. She will do whatever is necessary to attain that position. While she will show generosity, it must be done when others are present. She will treat others with kindness and try to form and keep friendships. However, her inability and unwillingness to show empathy for others combined with her constant attempts make herself the victim will make it difficult for companies to sustain.

The Overt Narcissist

In direct contrast with the covert, loud narcissists, the overt is loud. The overt, sometimes called grandiose, personality narcissist has a deep-seated belief that he is greater than all others. He knows he is superior and seeks power above all others. He wants to be in positions of power and management, and will make others suffer for it.

He is not interested in the thoughts of other people, or even the thoughts of others about him. He believes that those who look down at him are too stupid or incompetent for him to see the worth behind them. Their inability recognize greatness when faced in the face renders them unworthy of respect.

The loud, narcissistic narcissist is loud. He will not hesitate to proclaim his superiority. He might talk down to the waiter at restaurants, believing that he should have gone back to school if the waiter is to be treated with respect. He might toss the money that he used for grocery shopping on the counter and ask the cashier to take it. It is her job, so he shouldn't be doing her job. He may shout loudly that the grocery store bagger must be dumb if he is unable to separate his breads from his oranges. The bagger will not be allowed to speak a word about it. The narcissist will retort any evidence that he's superior.

This person is generally more irritating to be around than the covert-narcissist. Similar to the joke that you can tell when someone is vegan because they will say it to you, the Narcissist will reveal his actions or words as proof of his narcissism.

Overt narcissists often develop this type of personality because they have been told repeatedly in childhood that they are better than everyone else. He might have grown up rich and had a constant supply of domestic help. Perhaps he believed his superiority over everyone, in every way, because he could navigate school easily, doing better than all the other students, and always getting ahead in class. He will continue to act like that elsewhere. The result, regardless of the reason, is an arrogant individual who believes that he is somehow superior to others, even though everyone bleeds the same, eats the same and sleeps the same. He believes he is more powerful than others and regularly displays this belief.

The overt narcissist will often boast about his achievements and recent successes without ever having them compelled. He will talk about all the good things he has done recently and even exaggerate his involvement in projects and events to make him look better. He only cares about others' opinions of him if they are positive. All other comments will be ignored.

This behavior can also be seen in his relationships. He doesn't care what his partner thinks. He will not try to get his partner to fall in love beyond the initial love explosion stage. But what the narcissist really cares about, however, is whether he will continue to use her for his purposes. His romantic partners can only do good for him if they are used as tools. They are useful only when they follow his instructions. He will quickly dispose of any romantic partners who stray too far from the expectations he has for them and get a new partner.

An overt narcissist would never apologize to someone he perceives as inferior. It is possible for him to apologize to a peer or superior but this would be difficult. He doesn't see himself as anything more than an average plebian. He will deny any apology and, if pushed into a corner he might, just offer a quick, "I'm so sorry." This is not an apology. It only makes the problem worse. The narcissist doesn't have the right to control someone else's emotions.

The Toxic Narcissist

While covert narcissists and overt ones are complementary in the sense that some people are openly and loudly manipulative, while others remain confidential and sneak by unnoticed. However, toxic and toxic narcissists represent a whole new breed. These people and the phrase "people" are not meant to be used lightly. They are basically monsters dressed in human skins. They are cruel. The toxic narcissist would like to light a match so that the whole world can burn.

Chapter 3: What Is A Covert Narcissist

In this part we will describe narcissistic personality disorder. This will help you understand how your abuser might have got to where she is today. It is important to remember that most people suffering from a narcissistic personality disorders don't believe there are any issues. They rarely seek treatment. It is unlikely that they will seek treatment because you forced them to. Instead of trying to force your abuser into seeking treatment, it is recommended that you use this time to learn and understand.

Covert Narcissism - Causes

The exact cause of narcissistic personality disorder remains unknown. The majority of personality disorders are caused when there is a complex combination of issues that leads to the disorder. It is impossible to predict or predict if a child will become an narcissist. But there are some things that can be considered to help. Here are three theories on what contributes to the development of a Narcissist.

Theory One: Environment

Their environment is the most important factor. Psychologists and psychotherapists believe the environment of a child can have an impact on personality disorders like narcissistic personality syndrome. These disorders usually develop in the environment that surrounds the child, which is primarily in the relationship between the parents and the child. Narcissism can often be encouraged by too much praise or criticism. The child may learn the behavior from their parent and develop narcissistic patterns. Although the child may be on a narcissistic spectrum, they may not have a full-blown disorder.

Theory Two: Genetics

Personality disorders can be passed down from family members, just like many other diseases. An individual who is prone to becoming a narcissist later on in life may have one or more relatives with narcissistic personality disorders. Although it may be an inherited trait, there is no way to test genetics to see if someone is at risk.

Theory Three: Neurobiology

Neurobiology describes the link between the brain and behavior. Psychologists, neurologists and other researchers believe that individuals' neurobiology might encourage them to develop narcissistic personality disease at some time in their lives. Unfortunately, it is not possible to test a child for neurobiology in order to determine if they are susceptible to developing narcissistic personality syndrome. According to some theories, traumatic life events can cause neurobiological changes in an individual's brain that could make them more likely later on in life. This could be due to trauma itself or because the parent's behavior towards the child may change. The child may feel neglected by one or both of their parents if the parent's divorce is difficult. This could lead to narcissism. If the child suffers from a loss or personal trauma, such a serious illness or injury that leaves them with no other options, it could also lead to narcissism.

Risk Factors

Most people diagnosed with narcissistic personality syndrome are diagnosed as teens or early adults. Many will not get a diagnosis, believing that they are fine and others have the same problem. Some children, despite this being the age when it is most common for diagnosis and treatment, may develop narcissistic personality disorders as they get older. Some children may show narcissistic traits that are typical for their age. However, other children will.

Narcissism can happen to anyone, regardless of age, gender, religion or ethnic background. The individual is not the only one who suffers from the disorder.

According to psychologists and doctors, parenting is the main risk factor that can lead to narcissism later. Parents who neglect, abuse, are abusive, or otherwise pathological tend to be less supportive of their children. This can lead to them not realizing that they have a grand sense for themselves. Children should expect to be more self-indulgent. This is how they learn about themselves and how the world works. As they become older, the self-indulgence they feel should diminish. They are at greater risk of falling behind if they don't have access to healthy parenting. Instead, they use it to feel good despite the fact their parents are leading them into believing that they are not worthy or worthy of love.

Complications

Individuals with narcissistic personality dysfunction will likely face many challenges. Many of these complications can be traced back to social behavior. Individuals suffering from narcissistic personality syndrome may have trouble maintaining relationships, struggle at school and work, and resort to using drugs or alcohol. They are also more susceptible to depression and anxiety, as well suicidal or suicidal thoughts. One or more of these symptoms may be present if the personality is narcissistic is not treated. Because narcissists are often incapable of accepting and admitting that they are narcissistic, this is a common problem. It would mean that their entire life would be thrown into chaos. It's almost impossible for them to move from the self-serving lifestyle others feed off of and into one that requires their thoughts to be open to other people. They could feel more pain and losses than they are able to handle from this change. Narcissists may only seek help when they have lost their entire family and are no more able to lure people into their abuser cycle. Therapy may be an option for them in these cases. The therapy they receive is not guaranteed to work because they may be using this to make a deal and pretend that they are doing better.

Shame is another issue that narcissists must deal with. Every narcissist experiences shame in childhood because of how they were educated and their upbringing. This shame is caused by their childhood experiences. It depends on how they came to be narcissists, but almost all of them feel the need for a false self. This helps the narcissist get away from shameful aspects of themselves and creates a mask to cover up the problem.

The shame of the narcissist being raised in a poor home would extend to every facet of their lives. In this situation, the repeated feeling of shame and neglect in the child's life would cause them to feel traumatized. Their true self would be stripped away. The parts they felt ashamed of, or which they believe led to their neglect, would be replaced by a false self. This would eventually make them more appealing to others.

If the narcissist was raised in a home that was too coddled, any part of the child would feel shame. It would be embarrassing if the narcissist was viewed as an academic genius. Any struggle they had with something that made them feel like they were not competent or educated would result in shame. They would be addicted to the praise and attention that they received for living up to their parents' expectations. Any aspect of their life that was not in line with their parents' standards would make them feel ashamed. It could be those parts of themselves that didn't conform to what their parents are proud of, or aspects of themselves that were overlooked or punished by their parents. The true self would embrace all aspects of these traits, while the false selves would prefer to be completely likeable and admirable to parents.

A child may be ashamed if they were abused in their childhood. If the child experienced narcissistic abuse as well, this can increase and reinforce the shame. These aspects will generally relate to the abuse they felt. This could lead them to seek out a new version of themselves.

You can see, there are many issues that can occur when someone is ashamed of themselves. They blame the narcissist for the pain and trauma they suffered as children. This makes them feel compelled to suppress their true selves in order to gain more respect and better treatment. They are able to embody this false selves and feel that they are unique because, unlike other people, they have tried so hard to rid themselves of the "bad parts" of their identity.

Chapter 4: Narcissistic Abused Signs Of A Victim

Consider this: It has altered and damaged the whole reality. You've been humiliated and cheated, mocked, disowned, and even shouted at to believe that you see things. You thought you knew someone, but it was only a thousand pieces and your existence.

Your self-esteem has diminished. You have been admired, degraded, and then pushed from the platform. Maybe you've been supplanted and even disposed of a few more times. You may have been complicited and badgered over and over again to live with the victimizer.

This was not a normal divorce or relationship. It was an undercover operation to murder your reality and give you the illusion that all is well. You may not see any visible wounds, but the totality of what you have is broken pieces, recollections and inward traumas from war.

This is what narcissistic abuse looks like.

A dangerous narcissist's mental savagery can include physical and psychological mistreatments, toxic control. Stonewalling, misdirection. Triangulation is another example of the various terrorizing and violent methods. A person who is not compassionate, shows an excessive amount of privilege, and participates in social control to meet their own desires at the expense or others' interests, is what ends this.

Incessant abuse can cause PTSD or Complex PTSD in casualties. These symptoms may be exacerbated by extra injuries such as being abused by narcissistic guardians and/or the alleged "Narcissistic Abuse Syndrome" (Staggs (2016); Stailk 2017, 2017). Narcissistic maltreatment might result in sorrow, alarm and hyper-watchfulness. It may also cause a feeling of poisonous blame and pipedreams.

If we find ourselves in an ongoing pattern or misuse, it can be difficult to know what we are seeing. Victimizers are capable of creating a new reality for themselves, manipulating victims, and captivating them in love-shelling after any unfortunate events.

If you have experienced any of the side effects and have been in a bad relationship with someone else who is affronting and refuting you, then you might have been threatened.

1. Separation is an endurance instrument.

You feel detached, if not sincerely, from your environment. Dr. Van der Kolk (2015) says that separation is the manifestation of injury. The goal is for the emotions to be isolated and misshaped, so that they can live independently of each other. "Psyche desensitizing is possible even if you are in terrible situations. This allows you to change your reality. It can also allow you to overcome mental debilitating propensities, fixations and addictions. The oblivious can intellectually suppress the suffering so that you don't feel overwhelmed.

Johnston 2017, 2017. You may have hidden pieces of your baby that were never supported, annoyances and nauseates that you have toward your assailant, and parts of yourself that you are unable to communicate with them.

According to Rev. Sheri Hecker (2015) stated that "Coordinating and recuperating separated and repudiated character perspectives depends greatly on building a solid account that permits the osmosis a passionate, intellectual and physiological real factors." With the help of an injury-educated advisor, this interior mix can be achieved at its best.

2. Do not tread lightly

The most common side effect of an injury is to try and stop others from doing the same. It doesn't matter if they are your sweethearts, relatives, business partners, or friends, you need to be aware of what you're doing and how you interact with them in order to not get their fury, revenge, or become their object of envy.

It turns out that this does not work. The victimizer will continue to target you if they feel qualified for you to be their passionate punching box. You will become a constant restless in your efforts to incite your victimizer in every capacity. This is why you cannot showdown or set limits.

Outside of the abusive relationship, you can also increase your kin's satisfaction behavior, lose the will for being easygoing or emphatic while exploring the outside world with people such as your victimizer and badgering.

3. For the victimizer to be satisfied, it is best to put aside your most fundamental needs.

You may have lived a life that was full of life and purpose, but you no longer feel the need to live for others' needs. Once, everything seemed to revolve around the narcissist; now, your entire existence revolves around it.

In order to keep your victimizer's wife's happiness, you might have put your own desires, interests, and personal well-being second. You will soon recognize that the victim will never be truly happy with everything you do.

4. Dealing with mental illness and other medical issues

You may have gained or lost significant weight, developed extreme medical conditions that weren't there before and had to deal with untimely maturing physical manifestations. Your cortisol levels have become too high due to interminable maltreatment. You're no longer able to defend yourself against physical and mental illness (Bergland 2013, 2013).

When this happens, you are unable to rest, or you experience alarmingly bad dreams. You will then be able to recall the injury via passionate or visual flashbacks. This will return you to your original twisted location (Walker 2013, 2013).

5. The feeling of doubt is a constant.

Every person is at risk. If you see someone you once confided to, you will be more concerned about their goals. Hypervigilance can be described as ordinary alert. Because the manipulative villain has tried to say that your objective facts were bogus, it is difficult for you, or anyone else, to confide in you.

6. You have self-destructive or self-hurting thoughts.

It is possible to feel sadness, melancholy or tension. The conditions were so severe that it was impossible to move, even if you wanted to. A sense of learned weakness develops that makes you feel like you don't have to suffer another day. To adapt to change, you can also enjoy self-hurt.

Dr. McKeon, head of SAMHSA's self destruction prevention division (2014), stated that victims who are subject to intimate partner violence are twice the likely to try self destruction multiple times. This is how the perpetrators of murder commit crimes without any nature.

7. You can self-detach.

Victimizers tend to detach their victims. But survivors are also forbidden because they feel embarrassed by their maltreatment. Given the casualty allegations and incorrect assumptions surrounding mental and emotional brutality in the public gaze, survivors may be retraumatized even by law implementation, their relatives, and the collection of mistresses of the narcissist who may refute them recollections.

We fear they will not understand us or provide support, so we will avoid others to keep them from being victimized and avoid the possibility of retribution.

8. You are likely to find yourself comparing your self with others and censuring yourself for being treated badly.

A narcissistic victimizer is incredibly skilled in creating triangles or adoration for another person, or even carrying them into the relationship elements to make the victim more vulnerable. In this way, victims of narcissistic maltreatment may conceal the tension of being unfulfilled and may constantly try to get the support and consideration of their guilty counterparts.

A casualty in a stable, sound relationship may also question their accomplice's ability to treat other people with respect or compare them to others. This could lead them to wonder, "Why do you?" And then one is caught in a pit of self-accuse. It is true that although the accuser is the one who is to be held responsible, you are not bound for any abuse.

9. You will self-damage and be thrown into chaos.

Sometimes, casualties ponder about the brutality and hear that voice in their mind. This intensifies their negative self talk and self-harm tendencies. Harmful, narcissistic narcissists have 'code' for making their casualties reckless at the risk of driving them to self destruction.

As a result, the casualties are more inclined to take responsibility for their actions. We will ruin their dreams, their aspirations, their learning goals. The victimizer has given them a sense of helplessness and they accept that good things do not come easily.

10. You are afraid of what you love doing and not being successful.

Over-the-top predators often begrudge the prey they kill, so they get compensated. They make their victims blend in with their brutal and insensitive conduct. This control causes their casualties to hate achievement, as long as they're not subjected to censures and retaliation.

These casualties can be disillusioned, unstable, or lacking certainty and may escape the spotlight by urging their criminals to "take over" the show. You must understand that your victimizer doesn't undermine your endowments simply because you accept their second rate status.

11. You are your victimizer, and even a 'gaslighter' for yourself.

Legitimization, minimization, disavowal and mitigation of misuse are frequently victims'endurance tools in a damaging relationship. To lessen the cognitive cacophony emitted when you are abused or manipulated by an individual who professes to love you, victims of misuse are persuaded the victimizer isn't necessarily "such terrible" and that they probably did something to "incite" the maltreatment.

It is vital to reduce intellectual discord in the opposite direction by examining the personality of the Narcissist and their misuse. By understanding that the manipulative person is not the benevolent façade, you can find balance between the actual reality and the false self of the Narcissist.

The fact that casualty and victim are often in a tangled web of trouble is an indication that the casualty is informed to expect the victimizer's support (Carnes, 2015). Sometimes victims may try to shield their victims from legitimate outcomes. They might also show a positive picture of an internet-based relationship and compensate by sharing the responsibility.

I have been narcissistically treated. Do you know what's happening now?

If you feel like you are the only one in a relationship that is broken, it's not unusual to have others. You are not the only one. There have been many others who have gone through your situation. This type of mental suffering is universal and does not discriminate by sexual orientation, language or social class. It is essential to acknowledge and verify the truth of your situation.

You can begin to see the brutality in the events you've witnessed if you can. Talk about the realities with someone who can help you, such as a master of psychological well-being or someone who supports abusive behavior at your home, or family members. For example, injury concentrated yoga can be used to address similar areas of the mind, which are often affected by injuries (van der Kolk (2015)).

Support is available if you suffer from any of the above manifestations, and especially self-destructive thinking. Talk to an expert who is familiar with the symptoms of injury and can direct you. Prepare a plan of defense if the assailant causes you harm.

Due to the damage that the relationship can cause, the incredible injury bonds that can form, and the impact of injury, it is very difficult to break up with a destructive relationship. Co-parenting can be a difficult situation. You need to recognize that you have the option to move to No Contact and Low Contact. While it can be hard to rebound from this kind of misuse, it is worthwhile to do so and get the pieces back together.

Chapter 5: These Are The Things You Should Study

Sometimes, it might not always be possible to leave a narcissist. An adult child may have narcissistic qualities that a parent recognizes, but it might not be possible for the parent to end the relationship with the child. The spouse might not be willing leave their narcissistic partner because of financial or religious reasons. Although a child may recognize that their parent is a narcissist they might not be able to give up on them. These situations are all examples of why it is not possible for a parent to break off ties with a narcissist.

How can someone learn to deal with all the narcissistic qualities of an individual while still maintaining their sanity. How can you live with the manipulative, controlling, and even annoying ways that a narcissist uses? Here are a few tips that can help you deal with a controlling narcissist.

These are the Things You Should Study

You must learn to see the narcissist as someone else, not from their perspective. If this is impossible, none of the other tips will work. It will be easier to understand yourself and how to get away from the narcissist if you start looking at them objectively. Analyzing the behavior of a narcissist objectively will provide you with the insight you need to restore emotional balance.

Call Out

Narcissists often feel proud of their narcissism. You should call out the narcissist. If the narcissist is genuinely interested in the relationship, it will work. If this is the case, you can use a calm tone and not be sarcastic to tell the narcissist about their narcissism.

Cycle of Abuse

The narcissistic pattern of abuse is unique. There are four steps. The stages include: feeling threatened, victimizing others, feeling empowered and becoming the victim. Narcissists go through each of these stages frequently. Learn how to identify the different words and behaviors the narcissist uses during each stage. Once you are able to identify each of these stages, it will be easier to end the cycle.

Useful Techniques

Narcissists often become creatures of habit. If narcissists discover that a certain tactic of abuse works they will keep doing it again and again. Seven types of abuse can be applied to a person: verbal financial, emotional, verbal or sexual. Coercion, gaslighting (love bombarding), coercion, threats and manipulation of the facts are just some of the common tactics used to narcissists. Note all the tactics used to narcissists. Then, brainstorm possible countermeasures.

Play a game

Narcissists are known for using their charm to seduce others. They will ask them questions about other people. They are not interested in the answers and use it to talk about their own lives. Instead of being annoyed when they do this you could try this: You can play a game to see how quickly the topics change and how long it takes for each conversation to go by. It is important to keep the narcissist on the same topic throughout every conversation.

Be aware of unexpected surprises

Use the Trojan horse to warn you against narcissists. The Greek army attempted to infiltrate Troy's town without being noticed. They filled a massive wooden horse with gifts, as well as a secret army. The Greek army overtook the city once the horse had been under control. A narcissist's contribution must be treated with caution.

Take Care of Their Egos

To thrive, a narcissist will need lots of love, attention, affection and praise. By complimenting him, and feeding his fragile self-esteem, you can manage living with a narcissist. You have to be prepared for him to feed his ego. Otherwise, you will need to learn to manage his tantrums. If you are unable to leave the narcissist, then you must get used to it. It is possible to make a positive impact on a narcissist with just a few compliments. It's not manipulation. It is about understanding his personality disorder to be able to help smoothen things out.

Manage Your Expectations

Narcissists lack empathy. They expect sympathy from others but rarely receive it. Narcissists are unable to establish close and intimate relationships with other people because they lack empathy. You would do well to learn to accept and be at peace with this. Don't seek empathy or compassion from the Narcissist. Instead, manage your expectations.

Insecurities

Narcissists have many insecurities. They will be more defensive if you try to use their insecurities for retaliation. Instead, support them to safeguard their insecurities.

Boundaries Matter

It is essential to establish boundaries in order to avoid the blame-game. Narcissists won't apologize for their actions, but they will expect that you show humility. They might exaggerate the wrongs of others to decrease their own intensity. Instead, it's time to look at every mistake in context. Do not try to make them feel inferior while you are handling them.

Embarrassment

Narcissism is triggered by public humiliation. A narcissist is not capable of being publicly humiliated. You can stand with the person you are judging if they do something that might cause public embarrassment. A narcissist values loyalty, even when it is shown in times that are shameful. Try not to humiliate the narcissist.

You should look for good

A personality disorder is not a cause of evil. It simply distorts a person's perceptions of reality. Sometimes it is difficult for a narcissist to be positive. If you are trying to find a narcissist's interest, it is worth practicing. You can replace negative emotions about the Narcissist by something positive.

You need to decide for yourself whether or not you want the narcissist living in your life. If yes, you must be patient and immune to his negative characteristics.

Get your life back on track

It is important to understand that narcissists cannot be individuals who become afflicted by stress. Because of this, narcissism is also known as personality disorder. It's all they are, and not just what they do at times. Your traits of compassion and empathy are what the narcissistic spouse used against you. This part will teach you how to start the journey of recovery and get your lives back on track.

Set Boundaries

You must establish boundaries. A protective wall must be built around you if you want to heal. Your progress will be slowed down if you have negative memories about the narcissist or the relationship. Cut all ties with the Narcissist. You can remove the person from social media, your cell phone, or even an email address. All the items that could be used to identify you as a narcissist should be thrown away. It is time to let go of any ties with the narcissist.

Eliminate all Toxicity

It's time for you to rid yourself of all this toxic stuff so that your mind can be free from it. The best thing to do is to externalize it. It is possible to start keeping a journal and write about it. You can also talk to your friends, consult a therapist, and join a support groups. Because you can connect with others who have gone through what you went through, a support group can be a tremendous help.

Acknowledgment

Recognize the narcissistic abuses that you were subject to in your history. Recognize that the narcissist tried to hurt your conscience and with no remorse. It is important to understand that you weren't just manipulated, but also abuse. Your ability and willingness to suffer pain was used against yourself, and each cycle of abuse pushed you to the limits. The narcissist saw the good in him and ignored the warning signs.

Realization

It's likely that part of your brain knew that you were stuck with a toxic situation. You chose to ignore the little voice in your brain. Now it's time to take responsibility for what happened and to rationally analyse the situation. Perhaps you felt like something was amiss in the initial phase. You might have heard things from narcissists that didn't make sense. It is crucial to conduct a post-mortem investigation of the relationship. Now that you are aware of the red flags you ignored, it is time you look into them.

Self-inquiry

The wake-up bell for anyone who has suffered narcissistic abuse should be: Your vulnerabilities make your vulnerable to manipulation. You can identify your vulnerabilities if you do not want to be manipulated. There are common vulnerabilities, such as the need to have security, be loved and acknowledgement. These vulnerabilities could lead to manipulation if not fixed.

Healing

It is possible to heal your self by taking a trip down memory lane. It creates a sense that you are connected to your inner self and helps to resolve any unresolved conflicts. Narcissistic abuse of your inner child caused you to hurt. Your inner child requires your help to heal. Only when you are able to connect with your inner Child will you be capable of understanding the root of all fears and insecurities. You don't have to be childish. It's time for you to reconnect with your childlike nature. It is about reestablishing a relationship with your innocent and pure inner child. There are several ways that you can heal the inner child. You can say loving things to your inner Child and treat him with respect and love.

Focus

Sometimes your past draws you in. It is likely that cognitive discord and the trauma connection you shared with the Narcissist are the reasons for this feeling. This indicates that you may not be able to fully understand and process certain emotions. It is vital that you continue working to overcome any abuses you suffered. Instead of allowing your past to steal your present, set aside some time where you can reflect on it.

Be Patient

You have to be patient with yourself. Do not rush through your recovery. There will be moments when you feel like your life is in constant despair. It is important to remember that this does not mean you have to stop worrying about your problems.

Chapter 6: Five Things To Look For In The Narcissist's Marriage View

Wouldn't it be wonderful if everyone could be honest? Everyone should have a written message on their person that clarifies their intentions and motives. Pin badges that state, "I love psychotic games" and "I manipulate others" are not appropriate for interaction with Narcissists. If you're looking for something crazy. "Apply within" is a chaotic and profound self-exploration process that involves suffering, but which also teaches life-changing and important lessons.

But in the context of marriage and partner, the deceptions and games of a narcissist are not the best. Actually, there may not be any partnership at all. Perhaps it's only for a few moments. Partnership implies harmony, unity, trust, and mutual respect. All a narcissist can offer is their mind games, suffering, chaos, and oppression. It can be very oppressive to live with a Narcissist. They don't want to see you succeeding in your goals, dreams, or desires.

Let's begin by identifying 5 things to look out for before we dive into the 8 reasons why a Narcissist gets married.

Number 1 - The need to control

Narcissists tend to be extremely controllful. They see their partner merely as a supply or target for their deep-seated manipulations, control needs and desire to be in complete control. This can be easily detected and dealt with early. You might find it more difficult to recognize a narcissist if they have already lured you and wrapped their little finger around your finger. However, if this is something you can do from the beginning, then you won't have any trouble recognizing the sign.

This control can reflect in many areas. It can affect your choices in clothing, beliefs, daily habits, actions, likes and dislikes, or even your entire identity. Whatever the expression may sound, you are not allowed to be who you are or to choose your own path.

Number 2: Emotional Phobia

Narcissists are simply afraid of emotions. This does NOT refer to manipulating emotions or using them to cause harm or chaos. Instead, it refers only to real and genuine emotions and connections. Narcissists can't have real intimacy unlike in normal relationships, where love, affection and care are common. They view marriage as a way of gaining emotional dominance. While the narcissist might not be in any way emotionally superior to you, they may view themselves as being better than you. This is because they see emotions and vulnerability as weak and inferior.

Number 3 - A Fragmented Family history

It will always be possible to have some aspects of childhood trauma, family stories and repressions with your narcissistic lover. Most people see childhood wounds or family traumas as a way of self-development, healing and transcending childhood pains. But a narcissist will be so afraid of vulnerability that they won't even look to the bottom of themselves. Projection is the way your partner uses to hide their own issues. This can also include masking their inner securities or wounds with hurtful words, behavior, and negative displays.

You are your partner's scapegoat. They look for the same things you do, which perpetuates the cycles they are still trying to heal.

Number 4 - Projection: They As Their Mirror

You are their mirror. You are their mirror, or shield from their ignorance. Projection is an alternative to patience, understanding, compassion, and the desire to heal and help others. Imagine hitting a wall with a baseball. No matter how many times you throw the ball at the wall, it will always bounce right back. The ball is symbolic for the narcissists' motivations and inner turmoil. The wall represents you. You are just their structure and shield to bounce off. No matter the situation, story or negative trait you have, the narcissist sees you as someone they can trust to support them and take their stuff.

Number 5 - Insecurities masked as arrogance (and others less than desirable qualities)

It is when deep-seated insecurities begin to surface that you will recognize you are dealing with a Narcissist. These traits will always be disguised with arrogance or a false sense that they are superior, self-centeredness, inflated egos, and other less desirable personality characteristics. Unnatural and part of human nature, real displays of vulnerability, raw emotion and low feeling/moods will not be allowed. A need to seem all-knowing, superior, omniscient, and flawless covers many of the wounds, traumas or fears. In the narcissist's eyes, there is no room for healing. They want to convince you that they are perfect. Anything that threatens their self-created perfection is met with manipulation and projection-like tactics.

You are seen as less smart, less accomplished or less worthy by the narcissist in all areas.

8 Reasons why a Narcissist gets married

This leads us to the reason a narcissist is married. However, the truth will make you feel free and may even prevent you from getting married to a narcissist.

The Scapegoat

Unfortunately, you are their scapegoat. You are their mirror. You will be blamed on all the wrongdoings of the narcissist, judged and punished for their faults, mistakes, and other negative traits. This is how narcissists view marriage. They see their partner as a way of shifting blame and passing on responsibility. They actually need this, it is sad. They need to be with someone, and this is why they marry. Once they have found the perfect person, they will be enticed and seduced by their charms. It is obvious that someone who doesn't have Narcissistic Personity Disorder or can care for someone else, has compassion, kindness, patience, and a general sense 'niceness', will make the ideal scapegoat.

To Perpetuate Their Own Insecurities/ Traumas/Emotional Wounds

This may seem like something you would see in a drama film or psychological thriller. However, a narcissist getting married is not to hide their insecurities, traumas or wounds. It is important to remember that narcissists may have deep weaknesses they are afraid of admitting. Narcissists live in constant state of inner depress, chaos, and confusion. Their narcissism acts as a cover or shield that helps them hide their own wounds. As with all things in life we are social and family-oriented. (Yes, even narcissists!) This means they need to have someone to bounce off of, be with, as a support system and mirror. While the narcissist might not change their ways or wish to be healed or transcend their narcissistic ways of thinking, they will still need someone. They will always look to you for support, but you'll be drained and depleted.

To Keep Their Illusions in tact

They depend on you to keep them captivated by their manipulations and games. You can't have support or power without numbers. Your love and support can help the narcissist feel loved and accepted. Without support, there will be no acceptance. You cannot have something without energy, awareness, and support from others. We humans are responsible for creating and shaping reality as we see it. Because they know their illusions cannot survive without support, this is one of the reasons narcissists get married. Once again, you will become like their rock and gem. It may be unconscious, or based on your being fooled by their games. However, it is still a green sign.

For peers and colleagues

There is no better way to maintain your social illusions, charm, and eloquence than to have someone to talk to. A spouse or husband is the best way to keep a narcissist's personality and their self-made identity intact. The narcissist is normal to peers and colleagues when they have a rational partner. Their partner offers support, grounding and acceptance. The partner supports and defends the narcissist's narcissistic personality, and will also support it with love and compassion. It is almost as if the spouse or husband perpetuates their innate tendency to narcissism. This is the way a real marriage and partnership looks. You should support your partner and be there in times of crisis. However, it is not reciprocated. This leaves you believing that your partner can be charming and capable in real life of kindness, friendship, and social grace. Once you are again alone, they will play games with you and abuse you.

To their sense of success: Self identity and appearance

For their success, self identity, and appearance, they also require a partner. Your love, sanity, and professionalism will fuel your professional and personal life. Narcissists know that companionship and intimacy is a natural part of life. They make you look good by hiding behind your positive and beautiful qualities. It is a crucial part of their identity, public and professional/ private personas. Who would they be, if you withdrew support? They could come out as they really are or reveal their hidden motivations. A sane, sincere, and non-narcissistic partner can be the perfect shield.

"The Charm Illusion."

Many people won't choose a partner or a lifelong companion if they know they will be emotionally abusive, manipulative, and lack empathy. This is why a narcissist must have a husband or wife. Who would agree to be married to such a manipulative person? It is not possible. The charm illusion is what makes it all work. It's the perception that your partner is charming and sincere from the beginning. Why would others not see their wife or husband as loving, supportive, and kind if they see them as beautiful and worthy of a loving marriage? Support and love from friends, colleagues and peers is essential for a narcissist. Therefore, having yours will be the first and foremost step. Your support is like a cement, seed and anchor all in one. The narcissist would be nothing without you. "The charm illusion" is basically the lies and harmful stories your partner can share with you by accepting and providing compassionate, yet ultimately destructive, support.

To Have Control

As with the other things to be aware of, a controlling narcissist is one who needs to have complete control. Also, they need someone who can control them. While it might be hard to accept, you are ultimately their slave. Without someone to order, command, or control the illusions of the Narcissist start to fall apart. The illusions they have create a world that is not theirs. They need the false sense of superiority, dominance and control to keep it from falling apart. Whatever the size of their task, any feeling of control is fuel for their fire. The narcissist personality is characterized by a variety of traits and tendencies. Having someone to bounce around and control can help them expand their abilities and capabilities. If you are not willing to play along with their (often very sadistic) games, then how will they be able to maintain their illusion of control or "having it all together?" Their compliance is what makes it possible.

You Never have to Heal

One of the reasons narcissists get married is that they never need to heal because they have someone to bounce back on and project all their'stuff. You are their scapegoat and shield, rock, jewel, projection wall, foundation, and shield all in one. When a narcissist gets married, all of their unresolved traumas, past and present pains, sadistic and selfish traits and characteristics, as well personal issues, become accepted and integrated. Because they want to be their best selves before they commit to anyone, many people do the work prior to entering into a partnership. Many people aren't willing to let their past hurts be shared with their partners. It is a part of our lives to heal and develop ourselves.

The narcissist can find escape through marriage. They can escape their past, wounds, narcissism, and often 'evil' and sadistic intentions by having a life partner. They are incapable to have a healthy, intimate, cooperative, or supportive relationship. This is because they lack empathy and compassion. Even if your strength is beyond belief, you will still be the victim of the narcissist's inability to break down your heart repeatedly. Their inability, denial, and repression will cause you to be unhealed.

Narcissistic Cruelty while Being Kind to Everyone Else

This is the best way to approach the topic. You can look at Narcissus' mythological Greek tale. Narcissus was a son of the river God Cephissus. While many women fell in Love with Narcissus they found that he displayed indifference to their feelings and indifference. He loved being liked and sought after, but he was incapable of reciprocating others' affections. His narcissism eventually caused his demise.

This Greek mythological tale sums up exactly why narcissists so cruel. The love and affection you feel is what causes the cruelty you are subject to. Accepting this reality is hard and painful. But the more you accept it, and possibly incorporate the lessons from Narcissus, you'll be better able heal and move on. Like Narcissus and other narcissists who only love themselves in the eyes others see, so the love they have for each other sustains them. Narcissists have no affection for or feelings of love for themselves. They might actually hate themselves tremendously. This could be due to their self-deprecating egos, self flattery, arrogance, and self-denial.

Narcissists often have a unique self loathing that is hard to recognize and difficult to overcome. You are suffering from the effects of self-loathing and insecurities. Narcissists can make it seem quite the contrary with their strong self confidence and self assurance. However, they are afraid to face themselves. They are emotionally dead inside, unresponsive to love and incapable of intimacy and companionship. Mentally they are still trying to heal from the wounds and inner demons that have caused them. Your narcissist partner wants validation, admiration, approval. They secretly can't give it to themselves, no matter what delusions or false images they might present.

Projected cruelty and inner hurt will lead to real neglect and unappreciation of your love, support, and care. It can also result in an alienation from you and all that you stand for. Your patience, compassion, and special care will make you more vulnerable to their cruel and sadistic projections. All your attempts at companionship, intimacy, partnership and/or love are met with hate and compassion. People receive kindness. Or at least fake kindness. This is because they are so insecure inside and vulnerable that they need support and validation from others. If they were truly all alone and had no support, "friendship" or outside help, they would have the courage to examine their own reflection and face their inner demons. They then turn you into their main victim and target.

Chapter 7: How To Cultivate Self-Esteem, Self-Discipline And Other Superpowers

Maybe I wouldn't be going through the decade of hell that I did if someone had given me the advice in this chapter. I would have been able to fight back if I had known more about the power that self-esteem has on me. I instead ran headlong into a maze of insurmountable obstacles, motivated by my low level of confidence and discipline.

You don't have to experience the same stress if you can master your self-esteem as well as self-discipline.

What is Self-Esteem and How Can It Help You?

Self-esteem defines and determines your relationship with self. It is a measure of confidence in your capabilities and character. The self-esteem you have goes far beyond that. It is a key factor in your future plans, short-term decisions and how you interact with others. If you're going to get through a fight against a narcissist you must have incredible self-esteem.

A narcissist may find it difficult to attract a subject to his charm if the subject has high self-esteem and isn't affected by the narcissists' tricks. It is possible to rebuild your self-esteem and protect yourself against abuse from others.

Self-esteem is what narcissists want and lack. They have low self-esteem and have an unreasonable approach to filling that gap. Because of this, they can create idealized versions of themselves and the things they represent. To cope better with the feeling of emptiness or loneliness, they create a false identity.

Once you realize this, you'll understand why they constantly seek to destroy inner peace in anyone who is near them. They think and feel that they are not complete. They believe they do not deserve to be loved and appreciated. They attack others because they believe that they are not worthy of self-love and admiration. They aim to lower your self-esteem by using abuse, verbal insults and emotional conflict. But the worst part is that they are often successful in getting their victims to learn self-love. Narcissism is responsible for half the problems and pain that victims suffer. Unable to adjust to their new levels in self-esteem they either self-destruct, or even implode. This allows them the freedom to let their narcissistic partner take control of their emotional comfort.

It is crucial to learn not to lose your self-esteem. It is fine to lose some other things, but not your self-esteem. If you're in a relationship where self-esteem levels fluctuate, it can be devastating. Reality must remain true to who you are. Accept yourself unconditionally and love your body. Self-esteem is about being in harmony with and accepting of yourself. You will find it difficult to let anyone else in on the emotional serenity and grief you feel if you have a clear picture of who and what you are.

What is Self-Discipline?

In sufficient amounts, self-discipline should be a second superpower. Self-esteem is all about believing in your self. Discipline allows one to make decisions that allow them to get the best possible out of every situation. The basis of self discipline requires some psychology.

The mind of the human being is the largest organ in the body. It controls all actions and thoughts that we make, whether they are voluntary or not. It affects our moods, emotions and dispositions at all times. But, the human mind is somewhat wild. It seeks instant pleasure and gratification at all times. It default setting is always to search for immediate pleasure. It is because we prefer the easiest option to get our pleasure, like sleeping over working, playing tennis instead of mowing the yard, and so on. Unless there is some element of punishment or reward attached to not finishing a task, the simpler option will always prevail. This is not the right way to live. As you all know, it is crucial to put in the work now and enjoy later. Many times, we must complete our tasks today to receive greater rewards later. Many suffer from the inability of sacrificing time and effort now to receive greater rewards later.

This is where discipline can help. Self-discipline allows one to make more difficult decisions now in order to reap greater rewards later. It is common for people to associate self discipline with a life without pleasure. There is nothing more false than this!

Self-discipline shows your strength and control over what you choose. Self-discipline means that you are confident in your ability to control your life and that it is possible to continue that control. It is a declaration that you have control over your future and choices, and it shows your willingness and ability to live your best life. If you work self-discipline to your daily life, it will almost impossible not to display the best of qualities. The best thing about discipline is that it almost always walks around[T22] with positivity, resilience, optimism, confidence, resourcefulness and self-improvement. When self-discipline becomes a habit, it will be a part of every pore in your life.

To resist narcissistic abuse, it is important to practice discipline. Why? Why? It's okay to admit that sometimes you will be misled by him. However, once in awhile you can work out a way to end the relationship. To guard yourself from such situations, discipline is an important tool. Self-discipline is a key to staying on the right path. Without discipline and rules that are clear and you can't let go, you will sink under the weight of the narcissists' pressure. [T23]

These are the essential tips to help you build self-discipline and regain your self-esteem.

1. Know Your Limitations & Weaknesses

Everyone has weaknesses and limitations. Everybody has weaknesses and limitations that prevent us from living the life we want. You are not the only person with this problem. You can recognize your weaknesses sooner than you think and then deal with them efficiently. Your weaknesses should not be magnified or made more serious than they actually are. If you're prone to anger flares, it is important to recognize this and get started on a plan to improve your situation. It is impossible to control anger if it is not obvious. Don't make it a point to beat yourself with that same sentiment. Accept that no one is perfect. There are always weaknesses we need to be aware of and overcome. You should not allow your weaknesses to be a cause for anxiety and instability. Don't allow your weaknesses to burden your mind.

2. Your Triggers Must Be Dismantled

What is the best approach to overcoming weaknesses and bad habits "Out of sight," can also refer to "out of head." Bad habits are all linked to triggers. Triggers can refer to a specific person or set of conditions, as well as a particular mood. One example is a relationship that you have with your drinking buddies. It is essential that you can learn to eliminate triggers and break bad habits. Your triggers should not be within reach. Keep them as far away as you can.

3. Long-term thinking

To be disciplined, you must be able to see the bigger picture and make informed decisions. Narcissistic abuse can be escaped by short-termism. If you take the time to look at the bigger picture in abusive relationships, you will realize the entire thing is out of order. Narcissists won't allow you to see the bigger picture. This is why they treat each conflict individually, rather than allowing you to make demands for their change.

4. Cure your procrastination

It is said that procrastination can be a time-thief. However, I am here to inform you that delay can cost more than time. It can ruin your peace and happiness. You might end up taking the wrong treatment and have a lot of unhealthy relationships. When it comes to relationships with chronic abusers, procrastination is a path to self-destruction. If you didn't act quickly after reading this book, it would be a waste of your time. If you're still struggling to overcome your procrastination problem, you might want to put the book down. There's no alternative to procrastination. Make a decision to immediately implement all tips that are available and to then actually do so. It is important to manage your time. To stay disciplined and organized, it is important to do the right thing at the right moment. Time management cannot be separated form discipline. Procrastination is a sign of poor time management. It will make it easier for you stay focused and true to your personal rules.

5. Create goals for yourself, and plans to meet them

Either you set goals or help other people to achieve theirs. You'll be shocked at the number of people who live each day without any concrete or tangible goals. This group cannot be afforded for another second. You must be able, at any time, to identify your short and long-term goals. It will give you clarity and help you get focused on a goal. Take an hour to list your goals. List them. Writing down a goal can give it life and form that will force you to pay closer attention.

Don't limit yourself to these goals. You must create a plan that matches each goal. You can also use pen to draw a plan. Also, mark potential problems with the plans. With a clear destination and a plan to get there, it is possible to channel your emotional reserve and to keep your plans on track.

6. Start small but keep your eyes open

There are many benefits to starting any task off with a big bang. Although it can bring you great wins, it can also make you feel like a failure. It is important to start small when learning something new, especially if it is your first time trying. If your initial attempts prove to be successful, you can move on and take more risky steps. Avoid putting your entire life at risk by approaching relationships, business and personal life as a gambler.

7. Be persistent

Perseverance means being able and able to resist negative situations and circumstances in order to stay true to your cause. The journey of life is not always easy. We will encounter difficult situations and obstacles that are too overwhelming for us to manage. These bad situations are inevitable. The key to getting through them is to be persistent and stay the course. The majority of the dead end situations you'll encounter are just there to test how resilient you are. They are meant to deter others who don't have the same goals. There is always light somewhere. There is nothing you can do but give up on your dreams and the people around. Fighting for anything worthwhile is what you have to do.

8. Live Healthy

Our body is our temple, and it deserves all the care and attention we can give. Our body is a container for all of our goals, aspirations and dreams. It is not possible to afford not to give your body the respect and care that it deserves. It would be a terrible mistake. Living a healthy life is a must if your goal is to stay fit and ready to face any challenges. It's not right to let your health drop below the optimal level for preventable reasons. Healthy eating, exercise, and enough rest can all work wonders if they are integrated into your daily routine.

9. Reward yourself as motivation

I discussed the mind's natural tendency to seek immediate gratification. There's no doubt that rewards can motivate people to do things they don't necessarily like. Offering yourself a reward is a clever way to modify this. You can link specific rewards to certain milestones. You can treat yourself to a day in the spa if the rest of the week is clean. If you do your best to keep to your fitness routine, you may be able to buy a new pair of boots.

10. The Role of Failure

Your failure is not a condemnation of your inability to succeed. Far from it. It is simply a call to action to make it better. Sometimes, failure might not be due to your mistakes. Allow small setbacks not to affect your long-term moods or your decisions. Do not let your abusive partner make you lose all of your confidence.

It is essential that you keep a healthy sense of self-esteem and are disciplined in your struggle to survive a narcissistic spouse. I've already mentioned that I experienced relapses of my motivation and drive when I was trying to leave my marriage. Before meeting my friend from high school, I had realized I needed an exit strategy. However, my plans seemed to disappear after only a few hours. Once, I managed to get up the courage and tell my partner that he was leaving me. He made a quick, sarcastic laugh, and then replied with "Who would accept you?" It was quite painful for me to hear that. I was angry and that made me more determined to end my marriage. I was back at work two days later and everything had been forgotten.

The statement was an indictment on my thinking, and it was what went through me when he said it. After being angry for a while I began to accept the situation. Because I wasn't sure what I wanted and because I didn't have the self-belief nor esteem to challenge his words I began to believe them. I was not very disciplined. I was unable to make a decision, and then stick with it. I was always changing my yes's into little no's.

It's impossible to continue on this difficult path. You have to make your case and take a stand. You must develop self-esteem, discipline, and a plan to stay on track.

Chapter 8: Nurture Mindfulness And Accept Your Emotions

Mindfulness is the ability of living in the present moment peacefully, accepting all things without judgement.

Narcissists often dwell on the past and continue to rehash it. They replay the negative experiences they had with certain people and then plan to make amends by being irrational next time. Narcissists spend their time worrying about the future and past. These thoughts cause irrational reactions to the present.

Maybe you behaved similarly in the past. If so, you may feel depressed and have made your life miserable. If that is the case, then please remember that the past cannot be changed.

Because that's where your life is, the only thing that matters is the present moment. You can make your present as beautiful and fulfilling as you like. Simply by being aware of yourself, being mindful in the present, and accepting your emotions, you can create the life you desire.

This chapter will describe strategies you can employ to do this:

Take it one minute at a.m.

It's easy for emotions to become agitated, to feel hurt and angry. You can get attached to these emotions for too much, and they will bring out the narcissist within you. It is best to approach each situation one at a.m. Let yourself be present in the now. Meditation is the best approach to developing this ability.

You don't have silence or to go outside for hours of meditation. It is enough to focus on the present moment for a few seconds at a stretch and gradually increase your mindfulness to build it up.

Here are some ways you can achieve this:

* Do not leave your current location. However, if you are in a crowd, please move on to the next one.

* Close your eyes. Now, focus your attention on your breath.

* The square breathing technique mentioned earlier can be used if you wish. However, if this feels difficult, you can just observe your breathe.

* Watch your breathing as it enters and slowly leaves your body. Pay attention to any sensations or movements in your body.

* You might wander off in thought. It is possible to think about being lonely, the loss of your spouse, how no one calls you anymore, and what you deserve. Recognize these thoughts and don't try to suppress them. If a thought comes to your attention, acknowledge it and then exhale deeply. Remember your commitment to relax, be in the now moment, and then return your

awareness gently to your body and the current moment.

* These conscious attempts will be made many times. It's okay.

* Continue to calmly tune your awareness to your breathing and body.

* After a few moments, get involved with your five senses. Take a look at something you are interested in. You could choose the curtains in your room, a scuffed tile on the floor, or even your hands. As many angles as you can, observe it calmly.

* Select something that you like to listen to, taste and smell. If you hear the clock ticking, imagine how it tastes. Or, if the clock is ticking, take a bite out of the chocolate and smell the air. Involving your senses with the experience allows you to be more involved and gives you a chance to let go of any past or future worries.

* Do this exercise 30 seconds to 5 mins if you are able. If it feels difficult to hold it for more than 30 seconds, break it up into three parts of 30 seconds each.

* After you are done with the meditation phase, close your eyes and allow your awareness to focus on the world around.

* Even though you may have to overcome the tendency to drift in thought, each session should make you feel more focused. You are the winner. You did well, mate.

So that you can engage in meditation every hour or less, set reminders throughout the day. It is important to stay present and aware by consciously trying to become more conscious of yourself.

Now is the time to bring this awareness into every aspect of your life.

Take part in the task

Narcissism should not be considered a death sentence. It is just like any other issue, challenge, or ailment that you face or have to treat, such as the flu, cold, fever, stress or anxiety.

You can become more narcissistic if you continue to dwell on unhealthy thoughts. They won't bother much if you don't allow them to take over.

You can make the most from the moment by immersing your self in tasks. If you don't worry too much about the negative, you can reduce your desire to engage with unhealthy behaviors.

We have discussed the importance of being more mindful of the present moment, your body, as well as the five senses. Incorporate this sense of awareness into daily routine tasks so you can perform them with full awareness.

Here are the steps:

* Be more thorough when preparing a presentation for your next meeting. Pay

close attention to the words that you use, the theme you choose and how your fingers move when you type. Also, pay attention to how the words are interpreted by your brain. You might be thinking about how a colleague opposed your ideas at a team meeting. Recognize that thought and bring it up in your work.

* Always make your coffee first, before moving on to any other tasks. After you have brewed your coffee, take a moment to watch your coffee maker make your coffee. Next, look at how your coffee drips into your cup. Slowly grab the cup and sip one small sips at a time. Also, pay attention to the texture, flavor and aroma of your food when you're eating.

* Clean the floor slowly with the mop.

* Take a single step on your evening stroll. Pay attention how you feel when your foot is raised and planted on the ground. Allow

the breeze to cool you down and allow it to wrap you in its gentleness.

Do whatever you do with more awareness and acceptance. Aggressive, narcissistic-related thoughts might attack you many times. Accept your feelings and learn to accept them. However, you should keep your focus on the present. Although it's a constant battle, this is how life is.

After several weeks of practicing this, your ability to pay attention and enjoy your tasks more will be apparent. This will allow you to feel more peaceful, calmer, and more focused.

Be aware of your emotions.

The mindfulness you have gained in the past weeks can be elevated by becoming more conscious of your emotions. Your emotions have an effect on your thoughts. This can influence your attitude, behavior and ultimately your decisions.

You have let your emotions and thoughts get in the way. Now that you feel more in control, it is time for you to change the course of events.

Here are the things that you should do regularly right now:

* Write down any strong emotions or thoughts that you notice, and then talk about them.

* Do not ignore the emotion or thought. You can use the "Why" technique to dig deeper and find the root cause of your problems. If you think that you are alone, ask yourself why. If the answer to this question is "because my family doesn't want you to see me", continue asking yourself why. Keep digging until you discover the root cause. The same goes for anger. Think about why you feel the way you do and then dig deeper to discover the cause.

* Perform this exercise multiple times throughout your day, especially before you

go to sleep. By doing so, you can reflect on the entire day and observe any upsetting or important emotions.

* You will soon find many causes and underlying causes for your narcissistic tendencies. Once you recognize that, you can start to address them slowly and work your way up to a better understanding of yourself. Your family members and friends may not be able to talk to you anymore because you're too controlling and don't listen. By being more open-minded and accepting, your mental and emotional stability will increase and you will be healthier.

Keep a log of your daily reflections so you can track your performance and observe your growth. Celebrate it to boost your motivation.

Accept your emotions. Treat them with kindness.

An emotion does not have to be good or worse. What matters is how we react. Anger is just plain old anger. Until you react to it, shout at someone and throw a glass at their heads, it becomes something else. If you react to it or plot to make your best friend miserable, envy is jealous.

Take a moment to become more aware and compassionate about your feelings and act with kindness.

It has happened to you, perhaps, that your anger doesn't go out of control simply because the emotion is "bad", but because you are too focused on it. An emotion can last 12 minutes on average. If you are patient with your angers, sadnesses, envys, happiness, surprise and fear (the fundamental emotions), they will recede without causing any inner turmoil and not causing you to act irrationally.

Even happiness can have negative effects on your health if you hold it for too long.

While you might feel excited about meeting someone on a date, later you will realize she is not the partner or friend that you desire. If she refuses to do what you want, this could trigger the narcissist inside you and restart the unhealthy relationship cycle.

Avoid reacting to your emotions or allowing them to torment you.

Here's how it works:

* Take deep breathes and observe your body attentively.

* You are likely to feel more emotional and even have more reactive urges.

* Don't be afraid to express your feelings of sadness, anger, or fear.

* Try not to succumb to the reactive urges as this happens. Instead, be present in the moment and pay attention to your thoughts. No matter if you feel like calling your ex-partner to apologize or sending her rude messages or hitting your head against

the wall in frustration, deepen your breaths and accept those urges.

* Within a few moments, your emotions will subdue and leave you feeling more relaxed.

* Think about how you feel when you feel calmer and are not feeling the effects of intense emotions. This is how your brain will teach you to listen to your emotions rather than reacting to them. Think calmly about the message you would like to send your ex-partner. The message should be thought out before you act. Think about what you could get in return and then move forward.

If you learn to respect your emotions and how they affect you, you will experience a greater sense of security as well as peace.

You should observe your emotions whenever you feel the urge or need to manipulate, abuse, control or control others. Once they subside, try to find out where they came from and then come up with a more rational solution. This strategy can help you remain calm and in charge without allowing narcissism get in the way.

Your achievements so far have been impressive, as evidenced by your progress records. Keep working on these strategies, and be more mindful of your own self. You can also work on some more practices to help you have happier relationships with your loved ones and live a life that is free from narcissism.

Let's get to it in the next chapter.

Chapter 9: Escaping The World And Healing

The most difficult thing we can do to heal from a narcissistic love is to escape. There are many emotional and psychological factors that can trap us in a relationship. Others may be afraid of being physically abused or manipulated by their narcissist. It can be challenging to have the ability break the trauma bonds, safely escape, regain one's independence and heal trauma.

Breaking the Trauma Bond

It can be difficult to get out of a relationship with an abusive narcissist because the victim has formed a trauma bond. Trauma bonding, a type of strong emotional attachment that is formed between an abuser and victim, is called trauma bonding. It is perpetuated and strengthened by the abuse cycle. Bonding, in itself, is healthy and normal under the right circumstances. However, the bonds formed in the context of abuse can be dangerous and traumatizing to the victim. This is because they consider it normal to have multiple bonds with people they have abused.

Beyond the trauma bond, brain damage can result from prolonged abuse. Complex Post-Traumatic Stress Disorder (CPTSD), which is the result of abuse, can be a common condition. CPTSD is a psychological disorder that is stored in multiple places throughout the brain. This makes it difficult to eliminate and release. This disorder can cause your brain to rewire, leading you to constantly live in a fight or flight state. CPTSD can be treated and managed. However, you may not be able to live your normal life again after a breakup or other abuse. CPTSD will rewire you brain. You will feel trapped and lose your quality of living.

A key part of ending an abusive relationship with someone is to break the trauma bonds.

It can be challenging, but it's possible. The first step is to decide that you want life to be based on reality and not in the lies of abuse. It begins by confronting all of your denials or illusions. This includes those made for you by the abuser, as well as the ones that you created for yourself. It is crucial that you recognize that this abuser is abusive and will not change. You can grieve this loss as it does feel real. You are losing someone whom you thought was your friend, but in reality you didn't.

Apart from choosing to live in reality, you must create boundaries. A no-contact boundary should exist between you and your abuser. You must not ever contact them. If you do have to keep them around, for example if you share custody of the children, keep it as minimal as possible and focus on only necessary topics. While it is difficult to break old habits and make changes, these are important. You may find it helpful to seek outside support in order to help you with the trauma bond and other aspects that remain in your brain. While healing takes time, professional support is very beneficial to your long-term health. You should always choose a trauma-informed therapist so that they truly understand what you are going through.

Also, you must understand that breaking down trauma bonds takes time. Be gentle with yourself and be patient. You must remember that the creation of the bond took time. It took time and effort to create, so it will take time to disintegrate and remove. You can stay focused and deliberate, but you should also be patient with yourself as well as any challenges.

Escape Safely

Before you decide to end a relationship, the first thing you need to know is that they will continue manipulating you. They will manipulate you into believing you are reacting excessively, blame your actions for all that occurred, and convince you that they love you and want to have you back. To get their victims back into their lives, an abuser will constantly make false promises of better times in the future. It is vital to recognize that you should never trust any statements made by an abuser. All they do is to manipulate your feelings and get you back in the relationship. Look at the big picture to understand the narcissists goal. It may take several rounds of the entire abuse-cycle to finally see the truth.

It is crucial that you do not give up on your dreams and allow yourself to feel the pain. While you might feel like you cannot do it, know that you can. Support from your loved ones, as well as trained therapists, can be very helpful. Instead of contacting the Narcissist in a moment, speak to a family member or a professional.

No Contact is an Extremely Important Factor

To be able to escape and stay away the narcissist, it is necessary to enforce 'No Contact'. This will ensure that there is a law that governs the No Contact order.

If you have ever had any contact with the Narcissist, you give them the ability to manipulate you and keep the relationship going longer. This will be true regardless of what you believe. Communicating with the narcissist is a way to manipulate you and draw you back in. When you communicate with the person you're allowing your own mind and logic to justify why you think it would be a good idea. You must realize that you're in a very vulnerable, weak moment. It is time to let go of the narcissist. Instead, you must focus on your recovery. You must refrain from calling them, except when it is absolutely necessary (e.g., if they have children). Even if your children are shared, you need to establish a clear schedule for communication between them.

If the narcissist attempts to lure you back in during the hoover stage, you should understand that they are trying to do so because they are lonely and want to exploit your personal needs. They are not genuine. They don't miss you, love or need you in the lives of their children, no matter what they may say. It can be difficult to comprehend and embrace this on an emotional level due to how they have abused you and led you on. Due to the many emotions that can arise whenever you feel the need or desire to contact them, having a trauma-informed psychotherapist and compassionate friends or family members to turn to will help you to avoid the narcissist.

No matter how much you want to leave the relationship, it is a temptation that will not be defeated. It is easy for your brain to replay good times and convince you that things may change the next time. Many victims will end up returning to a relationship only to find that they are not going back. This happens because of a trauma bond. It keeps you seeing the good in that person and justifying your return. The lies and manipulations you see are what you really are seeing. As a victim it can be extremely difficult to tell the difference. This is because you would have to admit that you were being fed lies by the narcissist about every aspect of your relationship. This, naturally, can be very difficult to admit and endure. This can lead PTSD complexes, making it extremely difficult for anyone to accept or leave.

The reason your No Contact order is so important is because the hoover phase and the idealization phase are so well-refined in a narcissist. If you already have severe mental damage from CPTSD or trauma bond, there is no other way to overcome it than to seek professional assistance and break contact. As a victim, your addiction to the idealization stage has made you a target. This is what drives you back and allows you to justify the rekindling. It's the desire for that special, deep, passionate, and tailor-made relationship. This type of love is uncommon in organic relationships. You have probably never seen anything like it. You get a rush of hormones dopamine, serotonin and this can make your brain feel euphoric. This can lead to a physical addiction. You become so addicted that you can't help but ignore the negative effects of the addiction.

Avoid contact with a narcissist after you leave a relationship. This is a crucial point that I cannot emphasize enough. You are at risk of "relapse" to the addictive behaviors in the relationship. This can be avoided by ending the relationship abruptly and not looking back.

You can heal from your narcissistic relationship

The healing process cannot be completed in any given time. The length of the healing process varies from one person. You have many options to facilitate healing. These techniques will greatly assist you in healing your brain from trauma. It is important to realize that healing trauma within your brain is a long and difficult process. Therefore, it is best to not attempt it alone. The best thing for your healing is to seek support. However, it is crucial that the support be empathetic, caring and invested in your well-being. When you're vulnerable, don't rush to get help.

Boundaries are essential. Set boundaries with your self and those around you. After being abused by a narcissist you will need to set boundaries so that you are no longer dependent on them. It's time for you to be a good example of saying no and being careful about who you invite into your life. Be selective with who you let into the life of your family.

Spend some time getting rid off the toxic aspects of your life. It is possible to seek out help from others, since you are likely to have been isolated during this time. Journaling, sharing your truth, and speaking to a trusted person can be helpful. It can be extremely therapeutic to release all that you have held onto.

After years of lying, it is vital that you allow yourself to be truthful with yourself. Also, forgive yourself. You must accept that you did not know what it was and be able to forgive yourself. Forgiving yourself should be a priority for all the negative things you think about yourself and your relationship. You know that you are capable of doing better. Abuse can be complicated.

It is crucial to do the hard work. We are often abused and can sustain a lot of internal damage. This is where it's possible to release your inner trauma and heal the wounds. Spend some time looking at what is broken in you and dealing with them one by one. Your therapist is a great help. They will listen to your pain and provide professional support when you need it. You may also be able to use spirituality or yoga to get closer to yourself. This will help you discover the hurtful parts of your past.

It is important to shift your focus when you are trying to heal from abuse. Focusing on the world around us and engaging in your reality is key to healing from abuse. Keep practicing engaging with the world around you slowly and be patient with your self. This is a time to work on rebuilding independence, being independent, being yourself, and not being abused. Now is the time to embrace and love those parts of yourself that were neglected for so long. Ask people what they are doing. Engage in the lives of those you love and start to integrate yourself with the world around.

It is time for self-love to be reintroduced.

Chapter 10: What Is Narcissism Causes?

Many factors can lead to a narcissistic personality condition, such as environmental and genetic factors. Environment factors believe that pathological narcissism can be caused by parents who believe in the superiority the narcissist and reward those characteristics that will lead to success.

Research has shown that the brains of narcissists are more neurotic than those of non-narcissistic individuals. The left anterior Insula, which is a section of the cerebral cortex that has significantly less gray matter in the narcissist, has significantly more gray matter. Their cerebral cortex also appears thinner than the non-narcissist. The cerebral cortex is the part in the brain responsible for regulating emotions. This means that at some point during pre-adolecense, the cerebral cortex of a narcissist had stopped growing. It is possible that the narcissist may have shut off their feelings at one point in order to protect themselves from abuse or neglect.

There is not consensus about the possible causes of narcissistic personality syndrome. But, the lack empathy, emotional or physical abuse of the parent towards the child appears to be a notable candidate.

Abuse of any sort, be it physical, emotional, sexual or verbal, over a long time period by a parent, spouse, or both can lead to severe mental and emotional damage in a child.

Theoretically speaking, the first thing that could lead to narcissism would be having been raised by a family that does not care enough about their child's needs. Disorganized attachment can lead to parents failing to recognize, name, or regulate the child's emotions, especially when they are excited. Because the child is left to develop, he or she may experience intense emotions that don't receive the right responses. This can lead to an affective dysfunctional mind.

As a child grows up, the child realizes that his parents can't support him or his self-esteem. The child becomes self-sufficient. Because of his disorganized childhood attachment, the narcissistic person avoids attachment in adulthood. In addition, he or she is constantly seeking attention and admiration.

Another theory that could explain the genesis and progression of narcissistic personality syndrome is that of the future Narcissist. This hypothesis considers the person who was raised by families where success and status are paramount and only those qualities are considered. While this is true, some behaviors are not considered or punished.

Psychologists agree with the conclusion that pathological narcissism can be traced back to early childhood and close relationships with fathers, especially in the father's. Twin research has proven that genetic factors also play a significant role in the development and progression of this mental disorder. The only factor that causes the disease is not an inherited trait.

Families are essential for the psychological development of a child during the early years of his/her life. The parents of narcissistic personalities disorder sufferers have had an effect on their early childhood development, which may have negatively affected their self-esteem or restricted individuality. Because there was no limit to parental authority, children were either unable to fulfill their specific needs or had to suppress them. As adults, they lack the ability to perceive their own needs and feelings.

Children are subject to abuse and neglect

NPD is often a result of a traumatized childhood that left an adult with the condition emotionally disabled. The most common form of trauma is some kind of abuse. It can be emotional, sexual or physical abuse. It can be emotional, physical or sexual abuse. Sometimes it is all three. It is usually committed by one or more of the following: a parent, both parents, or a relative. In certain cases, a child may be physically abused and then emotionally abused in the second parent.

Ofttimes, abusers neglect to meet the emotional needs their child and instead focus on the needs of the child's body (e.g. The abusers often ignore the emotional needs of their child and focus only on the material (food, shelter, clothing). This leaves the child to feel alone and unable to understand or comprehend why they are treated that way. When an abuse child grows up, it's often that they can no longer provide for their own emotional needs.

Here, I would like to point out that the narcissistic parents do feel love for their children and have a strong connection. The bond between the parents is weak. The narcissistic parent puts their own needs first, even their children's. A narcissist has no deep feelings of love for any person and is unable to love their children and take care of their entire development. Although they often communicate their love to their children, they do not understand that they are incapable of loving their children and anyone else as deeply as other narcissists.

Children feel abandoned by their narcissistic parent, and are often left feeling unloved. This can lead the child to want acceptance and love from their narcissistic father or mother, but it is unlikely they will ever receive it. The narcissistic parent has suppressed their emotions of love to the point that they no longer feel any deep love or empathy for anyone else.

Narcissistic parents see their children and sometimes their spouse as possessions, and not humans. The narcissistic parent treats their family as a possession or pet.

A traumatized childhood can trigger pathological narcissism

A disturbed self image that is a result of abuse or neglect by their parents can contrast with one that is developed from pampering and excessive admiration during childhood. Narcissistic personality disorders can also be caused by this. Many people with this condition grow up with an overdominant mother, or with a dysfunctional relationship between their parents. Children who have a constant experience of exaggerated love and care from parents and are continually kept out of any difficult situations are also subject to restrictions in healthy development.

Children are not taught to overcome defeats in everyday life, school and in relationships with others if they become obsessed by admiration or preference. They become adults who are incapable of seeing problems as problems but can only help themselves when they need to find solutions or compromise. As the parent who is the most critical figure in the family's lives, the child often cannot reflect the behavior of its parents and does not develop social resonance. As such, the child cannot learn respect for others and feels superior in social interaction. Because this negative self-image does not reflect reality, it causes significant problems in relationships and eventually social isolation for those affected.

Roots of childhood Narcissism

There are many factors that can influence a child's development into an adult narcissist. It is possible for a child to become narcissistic if they are not given enough love and attention, or are constantly being criticized by their parents for poor performance. The children put their performance in the front and highlight that they are great performers to compensate. They hope this will give them the recognition they desire and the attention they require.

Too much recognition could also encourage narcissism

Therapists believe that too many love and appreciation can encourage narcissism. It can be just as harmful for children if their parents are their center of attention.

Children who are continually admired and treated with love and appreciation will have a hard time developing healthy self-esteem. You could be more susceptible for narcissistic personality problems.

Parents who love too much or are not loving enough to their children will not be able to satisfy their child's love and affection needs. Children require boundaries in order to have love. To grow well, children need to be able learn how to handle disappointments, accept help from others, and withdraw when necessary.

Genetic factors that lead to narcissistic personality syndrome

Twin studies show that genetic factors play more of a role in narcissism then in any other personality disorder. We don't know how the genetic factors can influence the development a narcissistic personality disorders. How they handle external stimuli and the way they process them plays an important role in their genetic disposition. Every child treats neglect and care differently. The child's self-esteem may be low at birth. Love and recognition can help to strengthen it. But, degrading or loving someone else will make it even worse.

Chapter 11: Codependency

Since almost 40 years, codependency is a term that has been used. Although codependency was first used to describe intoxicated couple, then called co-alcoholics. However, research showed that the majority of people who suffer from codependency are more common than expected. Our research showed that codependency is more common in those who grew up in dysfunctional homes or with a sick parent. This doesn't necessarily mean that you are bad. America's most dysfunctional families mean that almost everybody is covered. They found that codependency symptoms, if not treated, can become worse. However, the good news is that they can be reversed.

This is not a sign they have to be codependent.

Low self-esteem

Low self-esteem means feeling inadequate or compared to others. It's important to remember that self-esteem can sometimes be a facade. Some people are able to think positively about themselves. Others may feel extremely unlovable and incompetent. There are hidden feelings of shame that can hide from your consciousness. It doesn't matter if your life is perfect.

People like people

It is fine to want to please someone that you care about, but codependents are not likely to believe they have the option. For them, saying "no" can cause anxiety. Many codependents struggle to say "No!" to anyone. They are prone to neglect their own needs in order to satisfy others.

Poor Boundaries

Boundaries can be described as a imaginary line connecting you with others. Boundaries separate what you have from what someone else has. It applies to not only your body, money, possessions, but also to how you feel, think, and need. That's where codependents often get into trouble. We don't see the same thing. I feel responsible and accountable for the feelings and concerns of others, and I can blame someone else for my own.

Some codependents are unable to live without strict boundaries. They are difficult to open and close, so it is hard for others to touch them. Individuals will often switch between firm and soft boundaries.

Reactivity

You react to all the emotions and thoughts of others because you have poor boundaries. It is either a belief or defensive reaction when you disagree with something said by another person. Their words are endless and you just swallow them. A barrier would allow you to see that their view was your view and not that of you.

Caretaking

If you have weak limits, the consequence is that you will want to support someone you disagree with until you are ready to give up. Codependents place others before themselves. It is normal for people to feel empathy. It is possible to feel rejected if another person refuses assistance. They continue to seek out help for the other person, even when they are not able to offer it.

Control

You will feel more secure and protected with codependents when you use the command. Everyone needs to be able to control the events in their lives. Control is essential to avoid living in chaos and constant uncertainty. However, it limits your ability and willingness to take risks as well as your ability to communicate your feelings to others. Sometimes they are able to control their anxiety through an addiction, such a alcoholism.

Because codependents are dependent on others, they must be in control of their closest friends. This ability can be used to manipulate people and give them pleasure and care. Codependents can be controlling, and they will also tell you what to do. This is a violation the boundary of another.

Dysfunctional communication

Codependents can have trouble communicating their thoughts, feelings and needs. This is a problem when you don't know what you feel, think or need. Although it can happen sometimes, you don't have to be the one who creates your reality. You are scared to be vulnerable because you don't want to offend anyone else. Instead of saying, "I don't love that," you can pretend it's all right or tell someone how to proceed. Insecure people can be manipulative and frustrating if they are being manipulated.

Obsessions

Codependents may think of other people and relationships at the same time. This is because of their dependence on other people and their fears and anxieties. Fear of making or committing a "mistake" can also cause you to be distracted. You might find it easy to fall into fantasies about your ideal life or someone you love, in order to avoid the discomfort and pain of the present.

Dependency

They need someone to trust and like them in order to feel happy with themselves. Because they feel alone or depressed if they are left on their own, others need to be there for them. Even if the marriage was violent or traumatizing, it is difficult for them to end a relationship. They are finally stuck.

Denial

The problem with seeking treatment for codependency is the fact that people are avoiding it. It means that they are not confronting their problems. They think the problem is somewhere else. They then complain about or try to fix the problem, or they move on in their careers or relationships without ever realizing they have a problem.

The codependent suppresses their feelings, needs, and thoughts. They don't often know what they feel, and instead focus on what others feel. The same goes for their desires. They pay attention not to their own needs but those of others. We cannot deny their need to be independent and have space. While codependents may be vulnerable, some act as if the only thing they need is support. They don't want to help anyone. We accept their weaknesses, and they require affection and intimacy.

Problems with intimacy

While sexual dysfunction can be indicative of problems with intimacy, it is not what I mean by sex. It is being open and supportive in intimate relationships with others. Fear of being judged or dismissed can lead to you feeling afraid. However, you might be afraid of being smothered in a marriage and losing your freedom. While you may question the necessity of closeness and feel that your partner is demanding too much of your time, your partner may argue that you cannot.

Anxiety and sadness

Codependency causes stress and can cause painful emotions. Anxiety and fear are caused by low self-esteem and shame.

Anger, rage, anxiety, despair and hopelessness are some of the other symptoms. Sometimes, the feelings can make you feel numb.

You can get assistance with recovery and switch. It is important to be encouraged and guided in the first place. These are deep-rooted habits that are difficult to change. Get help from a counselor or join an Anonymous Codependents 12-step group. You can improve your self-esteem by working to become more assertive.

The term codependent is something that most people have heard, but aren't quite sure what it means. Many people mistakenly think that it means being too dependent or dependent in relationships. This applies mostly to girls, and especially romantic relationships. Some co-dependents may feel a need for or clinginess. However, that is not the best way to describe a relationship with co-dependent partners. Codependency can be more complex than just one or two characteristics. Some codependents do not need to be dependent at all and others may not show outward signs of dependency. This session is designed to give you a better understanding of the dynamics of codependent relationships.

The term codependent was coined relatively recently. It was popularized in the 1970s. But co-dependence has been around much longer. Alcoholics Anonymous appeared to be a support group for alcoholics. Some therapists noticed similar characteristics in many of their alcoholic parents. These family members spent a lot of time dealing with the issues of their loved ones. These family members were known to be co-alcoholics before the term was coined codependent. But it was later realized that to display codependent behaviors, a person doesn't need to be with an alcoholic.

It is possible to confuse codependency because it covers many unhealthy behavior patterns and thinking patterns. The following are the main characteristics of a codependent individual:

Instead of finding self-worth from within, you should use relationships as your source of self-worth.

Their time is spent fixing other people. This can be done by giving advice, forcing assistance, and so on. This can happen even if they don't want the help.

The bad thing about codependency? It's not possible for people with this condition to stay in relationships. Codependency cannot be reversed without a codependent making a change. The good news about codependency is that it is a learned behavior, which can also mean that it can be unlearned. The bad news about codependence is that it is impossible to change. He/she has to be open and honest about their marital problems and be willing to change.

It's important that you mention that codependents can be healthy. They are generally very caring, kind-hearted, and wonderful people. They often feel they are not worth caring about. If this sounds familiar, it is worth reading about the causes of codependency and what you can to do to make positive changes in you life.

Trauma Bonding

What is Trauma Bonding and how can it help you?

A trauma bond's toxicity is when a relationship makes you question whether it was passion or violence. This form of coercion is marked with repetitive behaviors where the narcissist abuses others, resulting in a difficult relationship.

Before we look at this cycle it is important that you understand that narcissists are not restricted to romantic relationships. In any adult-to-adult relationship, including those of supervisor and subordinate, teacher and pupil, and colleague-to-colleague, trauma bonding may occur as a result of mental or physical violence, to name a few. It includes both the relationships between parents or children as well other family relationships.

The narcissist process feeds an addictive desire to please their partner while also leading them to believe that all negative behaviors are natural. The process can be described in three stages: infatuation with the partner, devaluation, then fast dismissal. The cycle becomes deadly when the partner longs for the infatuation which marked the beginning the marriage. This leads them to forget easily, and they do whatever it takes to return to a place of good feelings.

Narcissists use inconsistent positive reinforcement to attract their partner. This vicious cycle often leads to an insatiable quest for the former love and admiration. The victim often feels too trapped to leave once awareness begins to kick in.

There are several ways to end an unhealthy relationship with a toxic partner.

No contact

Get away from your partner and have a total rest. You shouldn't be involved with your ex-partner. Don't ignore any post-separation email, text, call, or other means of communication. Yes, there was an initial spark that brought out the love, but the heart still remembers the beginnings of each cycle. Avoid sticking with old patterns.

Realize your life

Do not think about the past. Instead, live now and let go of any regrets. Be aware of how you are feeling at the moment. Healthy relationships do not leave people with feelings of devaluation and trapping.

Detachment

You can lean on and return to your dispassionate cognitive capabilities whenever distance makes it tempting to return to the relationship. Find out the core of your marriage. Encourage family and friends to share this information. This network will help to retrain the brain in much the same way that unreliable reinforcement is a learned behavior. It will be used in confusing times to protect your mental health.

Signs to be aware

Your potential romantic partner should not be able to show the strong characteristics of a paranoid romanticist. Avoid people who put a lot of focus on you, ask for grand gestures, rush emotional intimacy, or make you feel intimate. Pay attention how they talk about past relationships. Also, take note of other relational dynamics in the life.

Finally, consider speaking with a licensed therapist. He or she can help you identify potential risks and encourage self care as you navigate the complexities that come with dealing with this individual.

How to identify the Signs of Trauma Bonding

It is easy to confuse violence with love when you are dealing with pain and have not let go.

People who are trapped in a relationship of abuse are often mistakenly believed to be in love with the victim. Trauma can be overlooked when perpetrators are "caring" for one.

A lot of people in abusive relationships are unaware that they are experiencing trauma. They also feel the need to bond with it.

If you don't want to be loved, and misinterpret the signs as violence rather than affection, you could quickly become attracted to an abusive relationship. How do you know if there's a true love in your life or if you're stuck in a stressful fantasy of stress attachment?

Is this true love or abuse?

Do you remember falling in love fast and easy, only to have the relationship end in abusive ways? It was surprising to you that breaking free from toxic love can be difficult.

You see, there is something. Here are some tips to get rid this type of stronghold.

You must live a real life. You can't imagine what it might be or how it will be. Take a moment to think. Remember that you are committed to living in the present. Even if it doesn't happen suddenly, you can remember that your goal is to stop fantasizing and to live in reality.

Live in realtime It's about stopping and holding onto tomorrow's potential or actuality. Keep an eye on what's happening now. Be aware of the reasons you're stuck. Notice how hurtful you feel in this relationship. Also, notice how your self-esteem has been affected. Take care of yourself. Don't wait and hope. Instead, notice what's going on and how it affects me in real-time.

You can make one decision at once and take action every day. People can be afraid of thinking "all-or-nothing." Don't tell yourself, "I'll never talk to the toxic person ever again or worse." This is like trying to lose weight but convincing yourself that candy can't be eaten. Although you might be in an unhealthy situation, this doesn't mean you should make it a do-or die situation. Do not be afraid.

Only make decisions to support your self care. You should avoid making decisions that could hurt you. This also applies to emotional "relapses". If you feel weak, don't bother yourself emotionally. You can speak to yourself with compassion, empathy, and insight. Be aware that you are a piece of work and that life can be a journey. You cannot let your body beat you. Consider every interaction you have with the subject of your fascination. You must make choices that are best for you.

Start to feel the emotions. You can stop trying to reassure the toxic person when you are far from them in your life. Instead, you can write down your feelings. Anything that comes to mind, write it down. For instance, "I feel. I'm missing. I wish that I could be with you right now. Instead, I will sit down and write my thoughts. Instead of turning my back on others, I'm going learn how to feel the way through obsession. This can help you develop inner strength. Be open to your emotions and accept them. You don't need hide, run, hide, avoid, or give up on them. They will subside until they feel completely. Do not forget: this is your only way out.

Learn how grieve. To let go of a toxic relationship or to end a traumatic relationship is one of your most difficult tasks. It is impossible to live with reality if you don't recognize it.

Recognize the "catch" Identify exactly the thing you are missing. It could be a vision or a fantasy. Or it might just be an illusion. Perhaps your companion had convinced you that they could satisfy an intense unmet need. Once you've identified what the need is (or hook), you can move on to the mourning. Grieving means to open your arms (figuratively), and let go. You let go of the possibility that you won't ever be satisfied with your need. At the very least, you won't be able to meet this need.

Write down your top-line habits. Examples of possible examples: "(1) No one is going to call me names while I sleep. (2) I don't want to argue with someone drunk. (3) I will look after my finances. (4) I won't have conversations with anyone when it's too difficult, debilitating, or obsessive. "No matter what your concern is, find out what you can do about it to make them your ultimate.

You can build a life you love. As you start to imagine your future, both yourself and your children (if you have them), begin dreaming. You may be thinking about going to college, joining a church, starting a hobby or joining a club. Stop allowing negative relationships to ruin your peace and happiness.

Establish healthy relationships. You can only get rid off unhealthy connections by investing in healthier ones. Make sure you have a solid, close-knit, and connected relationship that isn't drama-focused. You should make your people the "go-to". Recovery can be very difficult without the support of others. Pay attention to the people you love. Stay connected with them whenever you can. If you require professional assistance, please reach out.

Chapter 12: Partner With Narcissism Tendencies

It's irritating to live with people who think that they know everything better than anyone else. Confidence in oneself is good and important, but there is a fine line between these two ideas. It is important to know this, rather than someone who thinks they know everything.

You can define a partner with narcissistic tendencies in two ways. You could find him suffering from narcissistic dysfunction. Or, another person could have similar characters to narcissists but not be a narcissist.

Narcissists, in general, are self-deprecating with a high level of self-esteem and anxiety. He is looking to be loved and valued for his inaction. It is a fact they won't openly admit they have, and that they need help. These tendencies, even though they may not be obvious at first glance, can lead to mental disorders or conditions if not addressed.

This disorder can have a negative impact on your relationships with people at work, in family, or in romantic relationships. This is why it is so important to recognize these tendencies in order to be able associate with them well and avoid the negative effects.

They love amplifying their accomplishments

If your partner enjoys exaggerating their accomplishments when they do, you should consider recognizing that this person may be narcissistic. But you need to be cautious about your judgment, as not all people who love exaggerating their achievements are narcissistic. When there is frequent exaggeration, this is the difference.

He does this to project his importance. He feels good about presenting himself as an important person. He is only claiming to be important, but this is not the truth.

He Uses Lies To Cover Up A Multitude Of Sin

Partner who have narcissistic tendencies are most likely infidels. They will lie to you to convince yourself that they are not infidels, and you might never meet someone like them.

Cheating makes them feel that cheating is the best thing to do for their partner. They fear losing their partner. This is the most common form of this disorder.

They are generous with their help

Narcissists will give advice when it is not necessary. If your partner shares the same characteristics, then you know that you are riding with a narcissist. It is an indication of their superiority that they ever do this. It has been said repeatedly that they give credit where credit is due.

Under normal circumstances, could you find someone who would also come to you, offer you guidance and support, but without any hidden motive?

They like to be associated with only good things

It is common for everyone to love and appreciate good things. You may reach a point in life when you simply cannot resist the opportunity to accept all that is presented. Narcissist tendencies make this impossible. They want to give the best to their partners even though it may not be possible. Their relationships are difficult because of this.

All these advancements are hidden plans to make people look good and be regarded as being of high social class. They say they won't settle for lower-class items or cheap stuff. This makes them very unhappy.

They Believe in Arrogance

They may be arrogant, but it is not their fault. They can be arrogant. They use arrogance to defend themselves. Your partner will not lose any battle to them, so if you act as if your partner is right, they may become arrogant to win and subdue. Sometimes, arrogance can be a gift that comes without condition.

Arrogance can only be accepted by narcissists who see it as a way to survive. In normal circumstances, arrogance is at a point when you feel that you cannot reach higher than this level. He amplifies his arrogance until it is too much.

Workaholism

Narcissists have this tendency. They believe in perfection. Because they believe in perfection, they will never trade their jobs for something else unless they have reached that level of perfection. Although managers are generally believers in perfection, they sometimes find it difficult to attain that level of perfection.

If perfection is part and parcel of a narcissist, it will be. They will not care about how much production is done in a company if they can achieve perfection. It's difficult to work with perfectionists in leadership roles. This leadership, however, will not allow for an increase in production. They get so impatient when things aren't going their way.

They love being social magnets

Although socializing with them isn't a common practice, it can be if they don't become the focus of the conversation. Talking to them will become a conversation about them. An individual with a narcissistic tendency cannot applaud another person.

Only praise and exalt people you want to, only if it is rooted in the person's (narcissists) effort. Then you are good to go. You won't be able to find time or attention from a narcissist who doesn't believe this. They believe they must receive all attention.

They Love Leadership Roles

It is not the topic of this article to discuss how they get to leadership. They love being referred, that's all you have to know. They will be successful if they can become a point of reference for others.

Even if they don't perform, it doesn't matter to them. As long they are at the top of their profession. Understanding that leaders are persuasive and very active is key, however, getting them out from that position is a responsibility for another day is essential.

Narcissistic people are usually driven to leadership positions. They might not be performers but they know that if risen to this level, they will be able control over others. This is what they do and die for.

Superiority Complex

He doesn't feel superior, but he does feel like he does. Their power is part. It is not necessary to present yourself as superior in a relationship. Although you might earn more than your partner, that doesn't mean that you have to be equal with them. This notion isn't just for the narcissists.

Narcissists exhibit power and control in their relationships. If you notice such behaviors in your relationship, it's likely that you are a narcissist. Do not ignore it.

The Tendency To Undermine Others

To subvert others implies that you are superior to them and that you can offer nothing of value to them. In fact, they may be a security risk. In order to achieve this aspect, one needs to be less concerned about how they hurt others.

He will try to use you to his selfish ends, and to your advantage. However, you are free to express yourself. You won't complain because you won't be given an opportunity to speak.

They do not have any intimate feelings about others

Their duty is not to sympathize with yours; rather, it is your responsibility to be sympathetic to them. This is a great quality for narcissists. If your partner is not understanding of you, then narcissism revolves entirely around you.

You can bear witness to the fact that empathy is a requirement in every relationship. There is no one who can give empathy to another person and not receive it back. If this is your case, then you must conclude that you live with a narcissist.

He will not want to adhere to the Set Rules

It doesn't make a difference what rules were established where, when, for whom, and how. He is the only one that matters. There are many rules to follow in life. These can range from the home to the workplace, the streets and the state. It is important to follow the rules.

This is a characteristic that narcissists have difficulty with. It's not possible for them be loyal and obey the law. When will they be heard? They are known for taking office stationery, refusing to attend appointments and disregarding traffic rules.

They do not have boundaries and are not restricted by anything

This person doesn't value people's contributions, whether they are physical, emotional or psychological. He likes to manipulate others without any guidance. He borrows money and does not want it to be repaid.

He doesn't show any mercy and is even more harsh on those he hurts. He instead blames others for their mistakes. He doesn't take responsibility for others' mistakes. He will not accept blames for the actions of his mate, even if they aren't remembered.

Ironically, he does many things

While she might make a decision to spend a lot on her makeup and hairstyles, it's not because she is rich or has enough money. However, her goal is to make high-class men jealous and be attractive to other women.

If you carefully consider this case, you might find other women applauding her smartness. While she may look happy, she will end the day bragging and nagging other women about how she deals expensive people. You might feel that all your applause was pointless.

They make good lures

They are charming as long they have a genuine interest in your life. They will make sure you feel like they are the only angels on earth. Without you, nothing can make it. Such praise is hard to give up. In fact, you'll feel extremely valued and special. This advancement could make you sick.

Wait until he takes you on, and then use you to his delight! You may be dropped as a rag. When he has an interest, he may make you a god. However, afterward, when you are no longer able to understand him, he becomes a difficult pill to swallow. When you think back to the whole experience, you will regret it and feel like giving up.

They need exemplary treatment

You will learn the most amazing treat from a narcissist partner when you meet them. You should not treat her the same as other people. They must receive immediate attention and be treated as urgently as possible. They won't appreciate it if they do not respond immediately to these requests. They believe that the world is only about them.

Chapter 13: Leaving The Abuses Of A Narcissist

Living your own life is the only way you can live a fulfilling life. Narcissists by nature cannot permit you to create your life. They expect you to conform to their worldview and take on their negative feelings. They serve them, they live for them, they do the things that are best for them according to their terms and conditions.

It is important to recognize that you may have additional obstacles to overcome if your abuser has been a narcissist. Emotional abuse can be very different from physical abuse. This trauma can cause different types of damage. Therefore, the treatment will differ.

What is the difference between them? What is the difference? You will be more programmed to engage in certain behaviours and narcissistic habits when you are emotionally abused. You are not only affected by the abuse, but also the distorted mentality you have.

First, get rid of all negative influences and surround yourself with people who are more healthy.

Healthy environments can give you new inspirations.

This is essential. Receiving contributions from other people will take away all the advanced techniques and tricks that narcissism can use, however many they may be. They only trust you to make them feel isolated and that you will be their only influence.

It's important to meet people with similar interests and to help you find them. You are encouraged to contribute from all angles and from all perspectives, provided that they are supportive and positive.

Another option is to try and reconnect with people who lost touch due to narcissism. People who are not a fan of the narcissist or who have been threatened by him, who don't agree with him and who refuse to allow him to be with them because he feels guilty when he does so. to work with them

This has many interesting facets. The narcissist can cause you to lose contact and interest in people you love.

Second, you may have lost touch with people you thought were important to you because the narcissistic group put you in contact with them. You would like it so you did. On the other side, you may discover that many of the people you did not like are now your friends.

If you contact them again, you will discover that they do not like you. They were also only recipients of narcissistic abuse. You may not know her but this is a good thing.

Today's people know things you don't enjoy and that aren't good news for you. These things will pass as you get better.

You are the boss of your schedule.

This is for two reasons. The first is that our schedules are based on our personal traits, lifestyle and preferences. Being responsible and making healthy decisions for yourself is key to being a responsible adult.

Being able to make the right decisions for yourself is essential for making wise decisions for others. How to support your loved ones or be a good friend.

The second, and perhaps the most important, is that narcissists have to control how their daily lives revolve around them. Their victory is any way they can dictate what you do and when they want.

This can mean that you may feel inclined to sacrifice what is important to you in order to provide for others.

You don't have to be selfish. But, I think it is important that you discover what you need in order to be happy and productive. What makes you happy? Not what can make you unhappy?

You should be able to make your own decisions and set your own schedule, with the events you choose.

A schedule is not an outline. This does not mean that you have time to schedule everything in hour-by-hour blocks. However you must understand the reasons behind doing something to avoid abuse and trauma. It is a form of escape or pleasure.

Keep track of your goals and what you are doing.

Do not be afraid to work with others.

It sounds like you are a police officer but it isn't. It is essential that you understand and accept the pain of abuse. You cannot run away. He would be willing to work alongside a specialist.

Why is this the final step? It's not a one-time step. This is because it is a process that must be continued through habit. It's about working in productive sessions. Recovery does not mean obsessing over the consequences of your abuse.

Recognizing abuse can help reduce its impact on your life. Tracking them down will help you to identify the source of the abuse and stop being a victim.

Most abusers will simply fall and "continue", or "get over" it. He does this at his own risk.

Do not allow emotional abuse to continue. It can cause severe emotional damage, and sometimes it can last a lifetime.

Do you want the debt to be paid off now, and in all the pain that it causes, or can it wait and be paid off later?

It is essential to recognize the severity and extent of the damage you have suffered and how it has affected your life. This will help you recover over the long-term. Do not allow yourself to be interrupted and sacrifice what is important to you.

I will also make it clear that professional visits are important and that you are exposed to people who care about their health and provide support for their personal lives. Both are priceless. These are even better when they are combined, and they can serve as a complement to each other.

To illustrate, if you keep your anger under control by scolding, but not by confronting the root causes, you will surrender to your abuse and turn your wheels. You will no longer be protected from your anger.

It creates a downward cycle, which continues, and it is based on the wrong feelings of foam and channeling. Instead of an upward cycle where you can recognize abuse and accept it.

The problem is that you may not be able to handle it. You might find yourself irritated by the abuse and don't know it. ,

It has to do primarily with you and not with them. Although there are many things narcissists can or should be responsible, their reaction is not one. You decide how you react to their behavior.

If you are able to solve the problem, you have to take full responsibility and not allow them feel bad. You were used to manipulate them into doing it. Now you have the power to stop.

While I did explain it in several steps, it is also an approach and way of thinking that can help you overcome the emotional abuse of a Narcissist. It comes in phases.

These steps will tell you how to speed up the healing process.

It is possible to abuse someone for a lifetime, depending on how long or severe it has been. But, it is never fatal. This is a common step that can be avoided in almost all cases.

Relax, if you feel that my personal experience can help, of course. Anything is possible if we have the will to make it better. However, it is something that you can make a decision to do.

Recognize the root cause and resolve it. But, it is possible to succumb to them and not even realize it. This makes feedback and conscious effort so crucial. It's important to recognize that this is an inevitable process and be able to accept it.

Conclusion

They can be difficult people to get along with. This type of personality is known for its self-centeredness and grandiosity. You've been devalued, idolized, taken for granted, and abused. Where are you going from here?

Covert Narcissism can be described as a condition that takes people's personhood away. It reduces everyone, including the narcissists and their loved ones, to objects with superficial characteristics. It is possible to find the real people behind projections. This is the only way to stop it. This book gave insight into how to better understand yourself and the person in your life who is narcissistic. It also provided data that will help you make an informed decision about how to proceed with that relationship.

This book provided the tools you needed to recognize hidden narcissistic behaviours and to unmask them. It covered setting boundaries and accepting vulnerability.

Narcissists use grandiosity in defense of vulnerability, shame, and insecurity. They try to project and deflect negative feelings onto others using denial and projection. While it may be tempting to project those negative emotions on the narcissist and cause more tension, it actually only makes things worse. Instead of fighting with the projections of the Narcissist, it is better to accept and acknowledge your vulnerabilities. You will be able to remain focused in response to narcissistic loss.

Narcissists are known for their self-centeredness and use exploitation, entitlement, and low empathy to mask deep feelings of despair. Narcissists, on an emotional and physical level, are desperate for your assistance. If they are allowed to eat your resources, you will be left with nothing. Protect your psychological and emotional space by setting boundaries. You should be assertive while keeping in mind differences between assertive, passive and aggressive behavior. Not getting too attached or dependent on the outcomes is perhaps the most important thing. Just be yourself. You have the right not to be respected by someone.

Finally, narcissists attempt to create an ideal exterior to counter their emotionally chaotic inside by using vanity. Narcissists often use the term of splitting to devalue themselves and the world. Because narcissists often have extreme thoughts or feelings, they can create similar thoughts and feelings in others. To avoid becoming entangled in the cycle of splitting, it is a good idea to be aware of your inner experience. Narcissism is a way to cut people into positive and negative pieces. You can only confront this by looking at people as a whole and complex individual.

Consider seeking support from others if you're determined to continue your work with the narcissist in thier life. If you need someone to remind you that it isn't all your fault, friends and family are great resources. You might also consider talking to a professional therapist. Therapy isn't limited to those suffering from severe mental disorders. Therapy can help you deal with stressful situations. Therapists can meet you at your level and offer you personalized feedback to help you better understand yourself. A good therapist will listen and give you feedback that is non-reactive. Sometimes, it takes several attempts to find the perfect match.

Therapy could be beneficial for the narcissist or narcissist you love. You should be careful not use therapy as a weapon. It's easy say something like "You really do need therapy!" or "You have some issues." It's a good idea to see a counselor. This is counterproductive since it reinforces the belief that therapy is only for crazy people. It also stigmatizes asking for help as something unworthy (and narcissists hate feeling shame). Instead, wait for a calm time and offer your support in an open-minded and caring manner. You could even say, "You know, I hear that you're feeling stressed lately. Do you think it might be worth seeking the support of a therapist?

You might feel more at ease talking to an expert.

The story of Narcissus was the beginning of this journey. This myth tragically led to him falling in love with an image of himself too ideal for the real world. Echo was equally tragic, and his voice was lost to the preoccupied Narcissus. Even though you might be playing the role of Echo, you don't have to allow your life to be dominated by Narcissus. Although it is difficult, it is possible for both of you to create enough space to allow the other person "show up." Even if you don't agree with the changes made by the narcissist, you have the power to make things better for yourself. This is sometimes a journey you and the narcissist can go on together. Sometimes it isn't. However, it doesn't matter what, remember your right of being heard, respected and seen.